The Recruiter Mindset

The Ultimate Guide to Working with Executive Search Recruiters

Written By
Mark S. James, CPC

The Recruiter Mindset

Copyright © 2024 Mark James

Published by Branded Expert Press

ISBN: 9798326377708

Legal Description

All Rights Reserved. No part of this publication may be reproduced in any form or by any means, including scanning, photocopying, or otherwise, without prior written permission of the copyright holder.

Disclaimer and Terms of Use: The Author and Publisher have strived to be as accurate and complete as possible in the creation of this book, notwithstanding the fact that they do not warrant or represent at any time that the contents within are accurate due to the rapidly changing nature of the Internet. While all attempts have been made to verify the information provided in this publication, the Author and Publisher assume no responsibility for errors, omissions, or contrary interpretations of the subject matter herein. Any perceived slights of specific persons, doctors, or organizations are unintentional. In practical advice books, income is not guaranteed like anything else in life. Readers are cautioned to rely on their judgment about their circumstances to act accordingly. This book is not intended for use as a source of legal, business, accounting, medical, or financial advice. All readers are advised to seek the services of competent legal, business, accounting, medical, and finance professionals.

Table of Contents

Forward v

Introduction... vii

Chapter 1: What Is A Headhunter? (Executive Recruiter) 1

Chapter 2: Create A Job Search Marketing Campaign™ (JSMP) 5

Chapter 3: 10 Recruiting Characteristics of Good Candidates 11

Chapter 4: Recruiter Preferred Resumes 15

Chapter 5: Get LinkedIn or Get Left Out 21

Chapter 6: Contacting Executive Search Firms....................................... 37

Chapter 7: When An Executive Recruiter Contacts You 43

Chapter 8: The Interview Mindset 47

Chapter 9: Closing the Deal: Salary Negotiation 69

Chapter 10: Offer Acceptance, Job Resignation, and Counteroffers.... .85

Chapter 11: New Job Assimilation (On-Boarding).................................. 95

Chapter 12: Lessons Learned on the Career Path to Success 107

Bonus Chapter: One Person's Journey 113

About Mark James, CPC 117

The Recruiter Mindset

Forward

If you are looking for the Holy Grail of secrets to successfully working with recruiters, Mark James is your Indiana Jones.

Mark knows the hidden traps that prevent the best candidates from finding the best opportunities. He also knows all the missteps that frequently reduce the potential compensation and opportunities for the new hire.

I've worked in and with the talent industry for over 35 years. Since the 1990s, I have been a colleague of Mark's and a close friend. I've worked with his clients, referred clients to him, and had intimate insight into his tactics and success in being that career sherpa to hundreds of his clients, whose lives were changed because they followed Mark's advice so well detailed here in The Recruiter Mindset.

In the late 80's, I worked with a national human resource consultancy that also handled some of the most challenging searches for the highest-echelon Fortune 500 talent. Our retainer search projects included the C-level, VP, GM, and product managers for some of the world's largest and most respected brands. I witnessed top-tier university MBAs snatch defeat from the jaws of victory because they didn't follow the insights you are about to read.

I have watched candidates with the rarest skills, education, and experience who have had fantastic success throughout their careers (perhaps much like you) slip on the proverbial banana peel while climbing the ladder of success. These missteps have cost many millions in potential earnings because they thought they knew it all.

Don't make that mistake. It's even more familiar with the top third of candidates than the mid-tier. Beware of your pride and read this book carefully.

Several aspects of Mark's career make him one of the best in the world to write this book. First, he has several decades of experience in recruiting and career coaching. He has worked with corporate clients from the Fortune 50 and smaller startups.

Mark has coached CEOs and professionals from all facets of an organization. He knows this space like few others. However, Mark also had a career in sales and marketing management. He has experienced managing one's career from all sides and has succeeded in every role he has taken.

Dear Reader, Mark James is a man who deeply cares and has dedicated his life to helping others. He is one of the straightest shooters I know. He knows from his vast experience that his insights will help you succeed. So do I. Mark is a winner. Pay attention to what he has shared in this book; you will, too.

Mark Faust
CEO, Echelon Management International

Introduction

In this practical guide, Mark James shares his knowledge of working with executive search recruiters during a job search campaign. This book delivers what only insiders know about navigating the job search and interviewing process to become a top hiring candidate. The Recruiter Mindset is designed to answer your job search questions and concerns concisely and efficiently.

This book is for people who suffer from job search and interview anxiety and are new to or overwhelmed by the process. Anyone privileged in choosing their career path is challenged with a shared burden, job search, and getting first interviews.

Whether you're a student, a recent graduate, someone making a mid-career move, or an executive at the career crossroads, knowing how to navigate the rough waters could make or break your career.

Knowing you are fully qualified for the job, have you ever envisioned your application stuck in a black hole? Have you ever wondered if you presented yourself correctly following an application submission or interview or could have done better? Both of these unknowns cause anxiety, which undoubtedly increases the probability of a negative outcome in your job search process.

Drawing examples from his 25 years as an Executive Search Recruiter and Career Transition Coach, Mark James shows readers how to put their best foot forward and get the job they deserve. The insights you're about to read have been proven to create positive results. Keep reading to stay in control of your career search. Each chapter will give you new tips as you endeavor to get the job you deserve and learn recruiter secrets to get the job you want.

The Recruiter Mindset

Chapter 1

What Is A Headhunter? (Executive Recruiter)

"We get too old soon and too late smart." Mark James

In other words, receiving an intelligent knowledge transfer is never too late.

There is an assertion that you need four things in life – a good accountant to manage your money, an excellent doctor to manage your health, a good lawyer to handle your legal affairs, and a seasoned and ethical recruiter to navigate through your career.

What exactly does a headhunter (executive recruiter) do?
Client companies pay an executive recruiter to recruit candidates with specific skill sets and experience. They evaluate and present people who match the company's performance requirements and, therefore, reduce their time commitment to finding and interviewing top-performing candidates. From the candidate's side, if they receive an interview with the recruiter's client, the percentage chance of receiving and accepting a job offer is remarkably better than through some other channels.

Why don't recruiters return my calls?
First and foremost, **Recruiters DO NOT find jobs for people – They find good people for good companies.**

Understand that many seasoned executive recruiters manage their business like a M.A.S.H. unit. Their days are prioritized to the max! If they returned every phone call, they would never get anything done. You may never know why if they cannot help you, don't specialize in your industry, or have a search assignment requiring your discipline and experience. There needs to be more time to reply to all the inquiries and unsolicited resumes recruiters receive daily. The bottom line is that you have no *"entitlement"* to a recruiter's time. That is, unless you are the perfect fit, the recruiter is searching for your type of skill and experience. In that case, consider it your lucky day when you get the call.

Why do companies use search firms?
- Confidentiality
- Not enough time to do it on their own
- Pressure to perform quickly without the right people
- Don't know competitor's people
- Recruiter specialty and expertise
- I Already tried and couldn't find high-caliber people
- No human resource department
- Under severe pressure to fill a key management position
- The company is budgeted annually to pay search fees to fill critical positions
- Positive experience with a recruiter (repeat client)

Should executive search firms be a part of my job search?
Yes, however, the most excellent chance of success still comes from your network of acquaintances, business associates, alumni, networking groups, people you know and trust, etc. However, search firms are working on search projects that need to be publicized or perhaps even known outside of the executive office. The recruiting industry is very harmonious. Most recruiters are affiliated with a professional network of other recruiters with specialties with many different search assignments. They exchange information on candidates and companies, resulting in split fee placements between search firms.

The Difference Between Retained and Contingency Recruiters

Retained vs. Contingent?
Like most industries, executive search has various companies

performing similar work but with different methods and results.

Retained firms are compensated on a progress basis as the search is performed. The client relationship is typically exclusive, with only one firm working on the search. Most senior-level executive positions are handled on an exclusive and retained basis.

Contingent firms earn a placement fee after the person they present is hired. The commitment between the client and some contingent search firms may be shallow, and some clients may use multiple recruiters to fill the same position. Most searches are handled on a contingent basis.

How do you work effectively with recruiters?
In your dealings with your accountant, doctor, and lawyer, you bring some aspects to the relationship that increase their abilities to address your needs and requirements. The same holds true with the recruiter as well:
- Don't try to work with too many in one region. DO NOT blast your emailed resume to hundreds of unknown recruiters. Use the **CALL* – SEND – CALL*** formula.
- **(*See cold-calling scripts in Chapter 6)**
- Determine the recruiter's specialty and the level of positions they place; if they can't help, ask about other recruiters who work with people within your discipline and industry.

<u>**Utilizing Executive Recruiters**</u>
- Provide a copy of your resume before going into your history. In your cover letter correspondence, indicate your salary history, geographic preferences, and desired position (based on your past performance and experience). Important: Know your professional objective—*ideal job.*
- Indicate that you are conducting an active search and request that your resume not be forwarded to any company without

discussing the position with you first. Always know who has your resume!
- Don't expect immediate results; it's a matter of timing. If the recruiter has relatable searches for you, they'll let you know. DO NOT pester a recruiter – it will only result in being blocked.
- Offer to meet in person with the recruiter; if they work with people in your field, they should want to get acquainted for consideration for current or future searches.

Questions to ask recruiters to qualify them before you send your resume.
- What industries do you specialize in?
- How many clients are you currently working with?
- How many open positions are you currently trying to fill?
- What kind of positions are you trying to fill?
- Do you work on a retained or contingent fee?
- How frequently should I contact you regarding open positions?

> **"Recruiters DO NOT find jobs for people – They find good people for good companies."**
> Mark James

Chapter 2

Create A Job Search Marketing Campaign™ (JSMP)

"If you don't have a plan – That is what you will get. Nothing!"
Mark James

Developing your **P.L.A.N.** is essential before executing a job search campaign. This is especially true when utilizing executive search firms and recruiters.

You have to know your answers to inevitable questions. Prepare to discuss your **PASSIONS, LESSONS, ACCOMPLISHMENTS,** and **NEEDS**. Once you are comfortable addressing these four areas, you will be on your way to eliminating the competition.

Developing Your Primary JSMP™ Statements and Documents

Creating your three **Job Search Marketing Plan JSMP™** primary statements is critical when answering key questions during the job interview. It will ensure that you are ready to confirm essential qualifications that support your professional objective and are reflected in the following communication tools:

- **Your Exit Statement** *(R.F.L. - Reason For Leaving your job or Reason For Looking for a new job)*
- **Your Positioning Statement** *(Career summary – known as the 2-minute elevator pitch)*
- **Your Professional Objective** *(What you are looking for in the ideal job)*
- **Your Accomplishment Statements** *(Defined as **"action=result bullets"** on your resume)*
- **Your Professional Resume and LinkedIn profile** *(To be professionally updated and optimized)*

The Recruiter Mindset

A Solid Communications Strategy:
- Presents an overall message to the person interviewing you and your target market
- delivers a consistent message of your highest and best use
- Demonstrates your competencies and skills required by target companies
- links you to your specific target industries and companies
- Counteracts real or perceived deficits in your abilities
- is reflected and confirmed on your professional resume

Your Career Objective:
- Defines what you want to do
- Gives direction to your search
- Forms the core of your **Job Search Marketing Plan**
- Provides an opportunity to explore your options
- Easily understood and focused

Key Areas to Assess:	Three Things to Remember:
What do you do best?	Things you can do?
What do you like to do?	Things you know?
What are your priorities in life and career?	Management roles you can perform?

Your Career Accomplishments:
Accomplishments (bullets on your resume) indicate one or more skills in action reflected by specific, clear, and quantifiable results in a story or example using a **C.A.R.** formatted statement. (**C**hallenge + **A**ction = **R**esult) Note: Only the **"Action=Result"** is to format bullet accomplishments on your resume. The **Challenge** is added as part of storytelling during a job interview. The **Challenge** can be any of the following: goal, problem, issue, crisis, obstacle, struggle, critical objective, etc.

Your Career Core Competencies

Competencies are the clusters of skills and personal characteristics that work in concert to enable you to perform certain kinds of work effectively.

Your Exit Statement

The exit statement answers, **"Why are you looking for a new job?"** or **"Why did you leave your last company?"** You can think of it as your press release communicating your reason for the change. It is a brief, non-defensive, positive statement that lets others know that your departure was not due to your fault. It must be understandable, believable, and credible, leaving no excuse for more penetrating questions!

Exit Statement Sample # 1: As a result of the merger of (new company) and (your company), 300 positions were eliminated, including mine. I am now exploring opportunities that fully utilize my extensive management and leadership experience and my technical and manufacturing background in the (types of industries).

Exit Statement Sample #2: Due to the recent reorganization at (company name), this has allowed me to explore new options. With my strong leadership record of improving profits, extending market penetration, developing new products and services, and managing significant containment, I aim to locate a position as an (inset discipline) in an international (industry) environment.

Exit Statement Sample #3: The recent acquisition of (your company) by (new company) created several duplicate functions and positions. Because of these duplications, several positions in senior management were eliminated, including mine. I look forward to joining a new (emerging trend/industry/venture) management team in the (type of industry). I know many of them will value my # years of experience in successfully (starting up/turning around) (new/struggling) companies.

Exit Statement Sample #4: I have enjoyed working with (your company); however, after (#) several years, I have decided to begin exploring new opportunities. With my strong leadership record of improving profits, extending market penetration, developing new products and services, and managing significant containment, I aim to locate a position as an (inset discipline) in an international (industry) environment.

Your Positioning Statement

Your positioning statement is a fundamental communications tool you will use in conversation throughout your job search in networking meetings and interviews. You will also use written versions of it in your cover letters and resume, which becomes the basis of your career summary statement. Your positioning statement responds to a request that you will frequently hear: **"Tell me about yourself?"** or *"What do you do for a living?"* or *"What is your Highest and Best use?"* It allows you to succinctly and positively position yourself in listeners' minds. Note: After you have composed and written your statement, practice it out loud (in front of a mirror) so that it comes out naturally and unrehearsed.

Use the following guidelines to compose your positioning statement and remember to keep it under 2 minutes maximum:

Profession:
I am an Information Technology Manager…
Expertise:
…with expertise in developing solutions through reengineering…
Types of Organizations:
…both in large insurance firms and as a consultant.
Unique Strengths:
I have been particularly successful in managing large IT budgets.

Position Statement Sample #1: I am a senior corporate officer with extensive expertise in operational management responsibilities, including P&L, strategic planning, and financial management. I have been particularly effective in increasing profitability, growing revenues, and managing costs. My organization showed solid incremental market share gains and maintained operational efficiencies. One of my key strengths is building management teams that value cross-functional working relationships.

Position Statement Sample #2: I am a senior executive with extensive experience acquiring and blending diverse or underperforming organizations into a strong and growing business. I've successfully developed and implemented strategic plans for business growth, cost engineering, and expansion into new competitive markets. In addition, I have a proven track record of establishing and building hands-on solid leadership teams and leading large organizations of people to meet company profitability goals.

Position Statement Sample #3 I am a senior management executive with extensive experience creating and blending technology solutions that positively impact and support business operations, sales, and revenue growth. My demonstrated successes have influenced vital business strategy directions and enhanced internal processes for new business segmentation, differentiation, and innovation. I have delivered a proven pragmatic business-focused approach to developing and leading strong technology teams with quantifiable and sustainable results.

Your Professional Objective

Your Professional Objective will result from examining your:
- **Career Vision**
- **Professional Values**

- **Skills & Competencies**
- **Career Goals and Interests**
- **Personal Characteristics**

The Professional Objective answers these questions: *"What is your ideal job?"* or *"What type of job are you looking for?"*

Use the sample statement below to define the ideal job you are most interested in.

Professional Objective Sample Statement
My professional objective is to be a (job title) in an (Industry) and/or (Project Management) environment that utilizes my ## years' experience in developing and executing _____ programs. My goal is to function as a senior executive using my broad experience and in-depth expertise in (your discipline) for a (size) company that is looking to grow and excel in its industry, and that is driven by its high regard for quality and customer satisfaction. I seek a corporate environment where mergers, acquisitions, or consolidation have created a need for new programs to strengthen the corporate image, build loyalty, and promote strategic business goals. I enjoy working in a team environment where quality, high standards, and professionalism are valued.

Five Active Lists to Maintain to Land a New Job

1. Personal and Professional Contacts
2. Target Industries and Companies
3. Executive Search Recruiters
4. Networking Events and One-to-one Meetings
5. Social Media *(Internet Job Posting Sites)*

Chapter 3

10 Recruiting Characteristics of Good Candidates

1. Can do the performance requirements of the job
2. Length of service at current/previous employer(s)
3. Changing job for good reasons other than money
4. Realistic salary and earnings expectations
5. Cooperative, positive, and confident
6. Reference and education verifiable
7. Professional appearance and attitude
8. Chemistry, personality, and cultural fit
9. Open to relocation
10. Has deliverables to sell the company:
    a) Your significant achievements? (Stories and Examples)
    b) **How** did you do it? (Predictive past performance)
    c) Can you do the job?
    d) Do you want the job?

The Ideal Candidate
A survey of 50 HR VPs and Directors determined the characteristics they look for in the "ideal" candidate for their firms.

The group discussion took on the following questions:
- What are the **"Ideal Characteristics"** you look for in candidates?
- What are some **"Red flags"** to look out for?
- If you had an ideal **"Ideal Wish List"** for candidates, what would it entail?

The group came back with some very insightful answers. Here are the results:

The Recruiter Mindset

IDEAL CHARACTERISTICS:
- Cultural fit to the company
- Strong (and proven) communication skills – Asks good questions, listens, and responds well.
- Can show initiative, enthusiasm, and confidence.
- Strong team player attitude
- Exhibits humility and understands the power of lessons learned.
- Strong set of technical and management skills for the position they are looking to fill.
- Willingness to accept responsibility and be accountable. Don't look to place blame on others.
- Shows the ability to be adaptable, flexible, and resourceful.
- Has a pattern of continued learning throughout their career?
- Most importantly, the candidate has **"Passion"** for the direction of where they are going or want to go!

RED FLAGS:
- Watch non-verbal cues during interviews and interactions. They often reveal candidates' "true" messages and/or feelings.
- Candidate is not prepared for the interview, the position, or knowledge of the company.
- Candidate is arrogant or cocky.
- Candidate is not a "hands-on" person.
- Candidate Makes negative and/or derogatory comments about former employers.
- Inconsistent on answers to questions or information on resume.
- Candidate shows no passion for what they do.
- Candidate does not know the ideal role they are seeking.

IDEAL WISH LIST:
- Candidates exhibit "active listening" to everyone they encounter during the recruiting process.

The Recruiter Mindset

- The candidate has a customer focus both internally and externally.
- The candidate has a skill set of "people skills" of empathy, passion, and development.
- Candidate looks to move the organization forward regardless of the "level" of their role.
- Candidates have a solid career vision for themselves.
- Candidate leads a balanced life with their work.
- **And the #1 Ideal Wish List Item:** Candidate has a proven track record of integrity, honesty, and ethics.

The Recruiter Mindset

Chapter 4

Recruiter Preferred Resumes

A recruiter, on average, will scan a resumé in six seconds or less.

If your resume appears the right fit, they'll continue reading it and consider calling you to conduct a phone or Zoom screen. This may lead to potentially handing it off to the hiring manager – which means you can get the job.

If they don't see a fit in those six seconds, your resumé will likely end up at the bottom of the pile—making your chances at the job nearly zero. So, those six seconds mean a lot. The key is writing a resumé that'll connect with recruiters then.

Key Tactics to Writing a Resumé Recruiters Will Read
In her course, O'Donnell listed several key tactics to make your resumé pass that six-second test. They are:

Show, don't tell.
Don't write "you are a strategic, innovative self-starter who loves collaboration" on your resumé. Instead, tell the facts that make that point. Write how you started your own company or launched a project. Or how you were in your company's top 5 percent of salespeople six years in a row. Or how you've been promoted at every job you've ever had. Those facts will impress recruiters far more than any adjective could.

List your skills at the top of the resumé.
Write your skills near the top of your resumé, even above your job history. This allows recruiters to quickly scan them to ensure you have what's needed to do the job. You want to list skills pertinent to the job

you are applying for.

Your work history on your resumé mirrors your work history on your LinkedIn profile. If these don't match up, it's a red flag, so make sure they do. Also, make sure your years of service are consistent. Listing years instead of months and years can imply that you're hiding something, like employment gaps. Avoid getting your resume rejected by adding the actual timeline to create less guesswork. If you did have a short stay at a company or two, feel free to add an explanation (such as if it was a consulting or interim role). Or, if your company was acquired or absorbed and you didn't change roles, make that clear.

Keep the margins wide and the font big.
You don't want your margins to be smaller than 0.8 inches or use a font less than 11. Why? First off, this will make your resumé more appealing to the eye. Second, the last thing the recruiter wants to do is squint to read your resume – that'll almost guarantee it doesn't get read.

But what if you can't fit everything? Then cut, cut, cut. This brings us to the next point.

For a resumé, less is often more.
You don't need to list every job you've ever had on your resumé. And you don't need to list every skill you've ever mastered. You need to put the skills you have mastered and the jobs you've had relevant to the job you are applying for on your resumé. Of course, you need enough to show you can do what's required to do the job. If a recruiter calls you and says, "Hi, I found you on LinkedIn, and I checked out your resumé, but I need more information," you know you've done this right.

Your Resume is a Marketing and Branding Document
Branding and Marketing yourself starts with your professional resume and optimized LinkedIn profile, as described in Chapter 5. Your goal is to secure the interview. When a recruiter receives your resume, they will assess if your resume convinces an employer that you are an excellent

competitive prospect for the position. Recruiters are compensated by the company when their client company successfully hires a candidate presented by the recruiter. As such, the quality of your resume directly affects their income, and they will not waste valuable time attempting to market a poorly organized and poorly written resume. When recruiters don't call you back, they usually feel they have a better chance of getting other job seekers to the interview table. Time is money for a recruiter, and an ineffective resume wastes valuable time.

As I mentioned, recruiters spend 5 to 7 seconds reviewing a resume before deciding whether or not it is worth their time. In such a scenario, it is crucial to ensure the most critical information is accessible immediately.

So when a recruiter is combing through resumes on Job Boards to find the perfect candidate, remember that hundreds of thousands of resumes are uploaded to Job Boards each week. This is your competition. Your resume has little time to deliver its substance and style to the reader.

Want a better shot at landing a job? Give recruiters' overworked eyes a rest. One of the easiest ways to impress these hard-working professionals is to submit a stellar resume with a brief cover letter.

Here are common resume pitfalls to avoid to stand out from your competition:

Boring Career Summaries
Your resume has to start strong, and a well-written career summary will almost always catch the eye of a seasoned recruiter, says Rachel Gauthier, vice president, practice leader, health care software and services with the Tolan Group, an executive search firm. That's because it's something simple that many job seekers don't get right.

The summary should not be overly creative but should be considered an elevator pitch. Think short sentences that show you've put some thought into your skills and experience—and be specific. For instance, compare these two statements:

"I'm a team player." OR *"I have a proven ability to effectively develop and lead teams in a start-up environment."*

It's obvious which is more compelling. If everyone else's career summary is day-old coffee, think of yours as a fresh shot of espresso.

Action = Result Bullet Structure

Instead of listing everyday duties and responsibilities as bullets, a better approach is to include quantifiable accomplishments. Focus on actions you contributed to leading to results. Example: **"Revised the supply chain order system by cutting expenses, which saved the company $30k a year."** This will help a recruiter and employer understand the value you can deliver. For positions that are harder to quantify, try to connect the dots as best as possible, such as **"Developed a new marketing plan that increased sales by 8%."** OR **"Helped transition data into the cloud, which made the organization more efficient and secure."**

Empty Buzzwords

Job seekers love using terms like "collaborative," "proven track record," and "what I bring to the table" without any context; these professional buzzwords don't have any real meaning to a recruiter. Add in some bullets that can show (rather than tell) the recruiter about your attributes, and back up your claims with results-driven examples. For instance, you can say you are collaborative if you also mention that you took the lead in helping several departments implement a new platform. Otherwise, you risk looking like you're spewing jargon just for the sake of it, and recruiters have zero time for that.

Careless Errors

Regarding resume writing, the little details can reveal how much effort you put in—or didn't. Executive recruiters review hundreds of resumes as part of their job, so it's only natural they will grow weary of seeing the same mistakes, outdated formats, and overall bad resumes daily. Many job seeker resumes contain spelling errors, typos, messed-up margins, odd spacing, and inconsistent font sizing. Not proofreading your resume translates into a lack of focus and reflects poor attention to detail.

Resume Formatting
Job seekers should stick to the grid and not be too creative or fancy when formatting (unless you're in a creative-type field where innovative flair and variable formats are welcomed). When in doubt, get a second pair of eyes to review your work. The bottom line is to get a free bacterial subscription to Grammarly.com. Some recruiters will offer suggestions to clean and improve your resume if they like you as a possible candidate for their search assignment. They can provide a format that includes a review of your resume's appearance and content and a prediction of a recruiter's first impression.

Preferred Resume Format
The resume format that recruiters generally prefer is the classic reverse-chronological order resume. The ideal resume utilizes limited space with the right font, spacing, margins, and properly placed content.

Creating a good resume is easy. There are many programs and templates to choose from. Whatever you pick, ensure it is Applicant Tracking Software (ATS) resume checker-friendly. The hard part is taking the time and effort to create a neat, polished document.

A proper format guide for a resume includes the following:
- **Template:** Top five include - Nanica, Primo, Cubic, Diamond, and Newcast.
- **Format:** the reverse-chronological format.
- **Section Headings:** Include your name and up-to-date contact information at the top so recruiters can quickly reach you.

- **Fonts:** Use professional, easy-to-read resume fonts. Use 14-16 pt for section headers and 12 pt for the rest of the text.
- **Margins:** Maintain 0.7 to 1" resume margins on all sides of the page.
- **Line Spacing:** stick with 1.15 line spacing.
- **Sections and Headers:** To make your resume easy to read and scan, use larger 14-font bolded section headers and plenty of white space.
- **Filetype:** Permanently save your resume format in PDF unless the job ad says otherwise.
- **Consistency:** Make sure everything matches in your resume formatting (e.g., stick to the exact dates of service and work history format)
- **Key Words:** Insert a 4-row by 3-column table of areas of your keywords included (Strengths or Expertise Included)

> **"The Resume should be written for the benefit of the reader, not the writer."**
> Mark James

Sample Resume Copies are available to download online at
https://hireconsulting.com/career-transition-resource-documents/

Chapter 5

Get LinkedIn or Get Left Out

It's been said that LinkedIn is the 800-pound gorilla. As of today, LinkedIn is the world's largest professional network, with 830 million members in more than 200 countries worldwide. My first exposure to LinkedIn began in 2003 when I was invited by a colleague to join. Back then, I was very skeptical. I didn't think it would last; it was just another social media fad. Boy, was I wrong! But I became one of the first 1.3 million subscribers.

In the beginning, I didn't embrace it. I wanted them to prove whether this was really to take flight. But after a while, I realized that people want, or even need, to connect. Within a year, I got my first 500 connections. I just languished around that for quite a while until I decided to start my own business. That's when I realized there's a whole new way to communicate with people you would never be able to reach. LinkedIn is the perfect tool for career management and consulting business management. It's the ideal arrow in the quiver for what I do and for millions of people planning to make a job change or trying to increase their visibility about being sought out by recruiters. Over the years, it's been proven that LinkedIn is the number one tool for recruiters. They use it almost exclusively as their database to locate, assess, and find job candidates.

When I first started, I didn't know the steps to make LinkedIn work for me. I underestimated its worth. Years later, I discovered the true power of LinkedIn. I was introduced to a self-taught LinkedIn expert and now longtime friend, Ted Robison, aka Mr. Link Me In, who showed me some tips and tricks to maximize my profile. He taught me about keywords, using the banner headline properly, and how to beef up my summary, add more substance, and gain more followers. Based on my keywords, my LinkedIn profile ranking went from page 26 to page 1. More on that later. Now, I consider myself a power user. I'm on it for at least an hour every day. First thing in the morning, I check the feed, which comes through based on the items that are getting attention. Here, you can comment, post your own, or hit the like button as often. Your participation is what gets you ranked higher. Your daily activity on LinkedIn will generate more views of your profile and potential connections to the people who view your profile.

Now, I can help my clients through LinkedIn. The first thing I do with any new client is to lay out the structure of how we will work together, which is processed in four separate phases. The first phase is administrative, preparing the strategy and plan for the job search campaign. We will first optimize the resume, perfect it for a professional job search campaign, and ensure that bullets are created as an action equaling a result - accomplishment statement. Once the resume is completed, we mirror it with their LinkedIn profile. This whole process is all about visibility and credibility. Suppose you look good on paper and social media (LinkedIn). In that case, it's a good bet that you will be a credible candidate for a potential job, whether a company, HR professional, or executive search recruiter finds you.

There used to be a stigma associated with bragging too much about your previous experiences. It's quite the opposite; the more you can project expertise, the more valuable it is throughout your career. Post engaging articles that are relevant to your industry. Once you optimize your profile correctly, you will get noticed and found.

As a recruiter, I have placed several unemployed people who had been out of work for good reasons. They just happened to be the best-qualified candidates who got the job offer from the pool of other people with jobs. It all boils down to who's qualified and who looks great on paper. It will get you noticed and hopefully lead to an interview. The final stages of the hiring process ultimately come down to *how well they like you. How well do you fit in or match with the existing team?* So, it's all about the likability factor, which I discussed in my first book.

LinkedIn also uses videos regularly, and I encourage my clients to use them on their profiles. When you upload on LinkedIn, it will give you extra visibility, awareness, and ranking. It's a great way to add more substance to your profile. Besides showing your expertise, it also shows that you're technologically savvy.

The key is to ramp up your visibility and ensure that people get your input. If they put something out there on their own, like it, comment on it, or put something out that you have created. If you see something on Forbes, Inc., Harvard Business Review, Wall Street Journal, or something significant to you, don't just share it. Throw an observation into the comment so people can see why you're posting it. Have your thoughts in the comments before people click the link to read it.

Pro Tip: Always research a person or company on LinkedIn. After that, I googled them. When I have a meeting, or I'm going to meet a new prospect, or I just met someone at an event, I want to see how they present themselves on LinkedIn. You can get many different types of information from LinkedIn if they've completed their profile, or you'll get nothing if they don't optimize it. Over 50% of job candidates were contacted a few years ago because of their social media profiles. I know that I don't even want to ask for a resume as a recruiter until I've looked at someone's LinkedIn profile online. Did I mention that almost 100% of all recruiting firms use LinkedIn as their primary database?

It is essential not to give too much publicity to your old company in your banner headline, which is a big mistake. It says, "People look at me, I work for IBM," or "Look at me. I'm a VP." They think they're being clever, but they are missing opportunities by not inserting their category of expertise, what is in it for the company, or what kind of service they provide. Your banner is the most valuable real estate. What do you do better than anyone on this side of the equator? People will pass you by if it's not clearly explained in your LinkedIn headline banner. You would think someone looking through profiles is looking for the right person. But it's been my experience that what they're looking for is a reason to disqualify you.

To reiterate, today's biggest organizational challenge globally is talent—finding, retaining, and optimizing it. A significant departure of Baby Boomer employees has begun to retire, moving to more flexible semi-retirement roles, i.e., consulting, fractional, and interim management jobs, or leaving the workplace altogether. Organizations need help retaining their talent, finding new talent to fill open roles, and ensuring they have the leadership they need to move forward. Many companies are turning to interim executives as a solution.

What's required: Clear differentiation and confident self-promotion.

To stand out in an increasingly competitive environment, you must become an expert at promoting yourself. And it goes beyond simply having a great resume and CV (although that's important, too). You also need to know how to stand out on the world's largest professional online networking platform—LinkedIn.

What To Say on LinkedIn When You've Been Laid Off?

Many laid-off people feel like crawling into a hole rather than broadcasting their new job status (or, more accurately, lack of job status) to the world. But if you want to find another position, that's precisely what you should do.

In the current economy, with so many talented people being let go, "absolutely no shame whatsoever" indicates that you are out of work. You exude confidence by not being ashamed that you're between jobs.

LinkedIn, an electronic resume, is a valuable tool to help you spread the word.

Until they are laid off, some folks either don't know how to use LinkedIn or have a very skeletal presence on the site. Perhaps they think of it as a job search tool (a mistaken assumption) and either aren't looking or don't want their bosses to think they are. Others are too busy.

Still, three years ago, senior people thought LinkedIn was for lower-level employees; now, everybody is connected and checking each other out. Often, the first thing people do when asked to interview someone – or even just network – is to look the person up on LinkedIn.

If you suddenly find yourself out of work, develop a robust, 100% complete LinkedIn profile. This site is so user-friendly that even newbies ought to be able to find their way. Those who need guidance can rely on LinkedIn's online tutorial or enlist help from an experienced friend or work colleague with a great optimized LinkedIn profile. When creating a new profile or editing your current one, be very public about the fact that you're looking for new opportunities. The following are issues to address in these **Key Sections of the LinkedIn Profile:**

Professional Headline
In this line, under your name, give a generic description of what you do or a sample job title (for example, Chief Administrative Officer, Chief Human Resources Officer). Label yourself as you would like to be rather than feeling limited by your last job title.

Current Position
Since you're now out of work, the "Current" heading should be deleted. Before you do that, though, cut and paste your previous company and job title into the "Past" section. Then click "edit" and "delete," and make the "Current" heading disappear. Don't be concerned that your job shows an end date. It's very acceptable to be in between jobs.

The Recruiter Mindset

Summary
In a couple of short paragraphs listing your core deliverables, emphasize your essential skills and examples of accomplishments. Conclude with a sentence, "I am currently looking for new opportunities in a couple of specific functions and industries."

When trying to fill positions that are now open, headhunters and in-house folks responsible for filling a job routinely comb LinkedIn for people who are out of work; it saves them the trouble of convincing someone currently employed to switch careers. So, indicating that you're open to new opportunities is beneficial.

For example, someone previously working as a chief administrative officer could write, "Actively pursuing chief administrative officer or chief human resources officer role in a dynamic, collaborative environment." An experienced broker looking to reposition his career into investor relations could say, "Currently seeking to leverage my Equity Floor experience and education into Investor Relations." (Alternatively, you can put "Actively seeking new opportunities" in your professional headline.)

Experience
Make sure your descriptions of past jobs adequately convey what you did. Standard resume writing rules apply here: use active verbs, describe your responsibilities, and show results. Since words are scarcer in social media, aim for punchy (think soundbite). Get recommendations from your current or most relevant jobs that reflect varying perspectives — for example, from a manager, a colleague, and a client.

Education
A perennial question is whether people should include graduation dates or a tip-off for their age. Executives between their mid-40s and early 60s are discouraged from trying to mask their age.

How do you know when you've finished? When you're in "Edit Profile" mode on LinkedIn, a metric shows the percent of profile completeness. It will suggest what you're missing — whether it's a photo or recommendations. Keep revising until you hit the 100% mark. Then, proofread diligently.

Once you have found another position, you'll no doubt be eager to update your LinkedIn profile to show where you've landed. But don't neglect it after that. This social media tool is great for sharing updates about what you are doing; your entries on the home page appear at the top of your profile. Think of your LinkedIn page as an active site. You don't want it to go stagnant.

10 Tips to Optimize Your LinkedIn Presence

If you want to land a new job and secure more consulting clients or interim/fractional management roles, you must be prominent on and active on the world's #1 social media site.

Here are the **Top Ten Ways to Optimize Your LinkedIn Presence:**

1. Know (and share) your story
What's your most remarkable talent? Your most valuable deliverable? The thing (or things) you do better than anyone else on this side of the equator? That's your "story," — and it needs to be communicated everywhere you promote yourself, especially on your LinkedIn profile.

2. Define your DNA
That means your **D**rive (what motivates you), your **N**iche (your exclusive area of focus), and your **A**ccomplishments (what sets you apart). Take time to describe how you got to where you are today and what you can do to satisfy a company's needs and wants.

3. Know your keywords
On LinkedIn, everything revolves around keywords. Whatever defines you (your expertise, deliverables, skill sets, unique value), use those keywords throughout your profile to get a higher ranking during a

search. Optimize those keywords by using them repeatedly in different sections.

4. Maximize your banner headline
Your banner headline used to be limited to 20 characters, but it's now been expanded to include more information. The more you can share your uniqueness and special skills in the headline, the better. Think about sharing a mantra, slogan, philosophy, or whatever you're passionate about.

5. Make (and build) thoughtful connections
When you meet new business colleagues, ask to connect with them on LinkedIn. If you get a connection request, make sure you know them or have a mutual connection. Don't just accept the connection automatically. Take time to introduce yourself and see if the connection is relevant. If so, accept the connection, but take it one step further by setting up a phone call or Zoom meeting to get to know each other and see how you can help each other.

6. Harness the power of groups
With the premium LinkedIn membership, you can join up to 50 different groups, including industry associations related to your field (e.g., finance, manufacturing, sales, marketing) or vertical markets you support. Review discussions and others' posts, and offer your perspective (see formula below).

7. Use the "5-3-1" daily activity formula
One of the best ways to boost your LinkedIn visibility is to take these actions every day (five days a week):

- ✓ **5 times a day:** "Like" something you see. Look for people who have posted something you like or agree/align with. Click the like button. It's a great way to get noticed and appreciated.
- ✓ **3 times a day:** "Comment" on a post you like. Share why you agree and how you can relate, or add another idea, suggestion, or tip.

- ✓ **1 time a day:** Post or share one thing new from you. It could be something you wrote or a relevant article you found elsewhere. Post it and comment on why it inspires you, why you agree, or any additional perspective that demonstrates your expertise. All your followers will see the activity, increasing your visibility as a subject matter expert or thought leader.

8. Be diligent and consistent
Commit to doing some activity on LinkedIn five days a week. The activities may be small, but they all increase visibility over time.

9. Get a professional headshot and a customized background image
Hire a professional photographer to create a "LinkedIn high-resolution headshot" and upload a "unique" banner cover picture behind your headshot at the top of your profile — something related to your industry or vertical market. A Google search will pull up hundreds of free options.

10. Build your bank of recommendations
Offer to recommend your clients, colleagues, or customers, then ask if they would be willing to return the favor. (Most will say yes.)

Biggest LinkedIn Mistakes

It's not only essential to know what to do on LinkedIn, but it's also important to know what not to do:

1. No Profile Photo
"An ounce of image is worth a pound of performance - and you only have 50 Milliseconds to make a first impression?"

The absence of a LinkedIn photo can be interpreted as "I'm too busy to take this seriously." Spend time and money on a professional headshot. And look the part—make sure you dress to impress for success.

The human brain processes images faster than words. According to HubSpot, the brain processes visual information 60,000 times faster than the time it takes for the brain to decode text. It does this in 1/10 of 1 second. Tie that into the impact you can make with a personal connection. Relationship building online depends on images.

In the internet age, most of the first impressions we make are now online. And that means that photography is more important to businesses than ever before! Visual consistency is the fastest way to tell your story and connect with recruiters, companies, and clients.

A headshot alone is not personal branding but will contribute to your brand. Take the time to get it done professionally. Your social media profile headshot photos should be close-up, recognizable images of you.

Update your LinkedIn banner cover photo. This is the background image at the top of your profile. Recruiters search hundreds of profiles, and your imagery might get their attention.

Solution: Here are 5 Key Elements of a Good LinkedIn Profile Picture:

- **Professionally taken photograph**
- **Professional attire and dress code**
- **Cheerful, optimistic, smile and attitude**
- **Current and recent photo**
- **Optimized headshot and resolution**

2. A boring introductory "Banner Headline"

This title appears right below your photo and name, making it one of the first things people see. Think of this field as your answer to "What do you do?" But **do not** list your job title! Your brief reply might be, "Manufacturing and Technology Leadership" OR "I bring next-generation products from design into the marketplace." To stand out, be creative and personalize your headline banner with a quote or slogan.

Solution: Your headline needs to answer three questions:

1) What do you do?
2) Who do you help?

3) How do you help them?

3. Maximize and Optimize your "About" summary

Like an entrepreneur pitching a startup or a writer trying to introduce a screenplay to a producer, you have an idea to sell. That idea is you.

Use first-person pronounces: It's okay to say "I" — people expect to hear from you directly. Referring to yourself in the third person is for the resume. Your LinkedIn profile should be more personal and strive to make connections. Avoid the over-used buzz phrases and cliches like: "What I bring to the table," I'm a team player who enjoys collaborating with others," OR "I am a people person who enjoys working with teams."

Solution: Go one step further by describing what being a "team player" means to you: *"I lead collaborative teams that bring out the best in others and myself to address problems and brainstorm solutions creatively."*

Instead of saying what you bring, try this; *"One of my greatest deliverables is my ability to lead teams; let me give you an example."*

Make it meaningful: While the content of your "About" statement makes it all about you, the connection it makes is all about others. The goal is to present and showcase WHO you are. Why do you do what you do? How are you successful? And WHAT is in it for your next employer?

4. Work Experience section without Substance

Just as with your resume, you should use an accomplishment-first approach. I suggest at least 3-5 action=result bullet accomplishments for every job you have listed on your LinkedIn profile.

Here is a good bullet structure sample: "Led a team of twelve colleagues in six countries in launching a new product line that exceeded initial sales projections by 18%."

Use the same approach for your past jobs, highlighting your top accomplishments. Share credit with your team: If you worked on a project with others, tag their names in your LinkedIn post (especially if you're a mid-level manager who directed the team while others did the work). This in no way dilutes recognition of your efforts.

Incorporate keywords relevant to your industry: Employers scan for keywords that indicate your skills and level of expertise. One way to identify these keywords is to read job descriptions in your industry and take note of specific qualifications. Then, make sure those exact phrases are included in your profile. Keep updating and refreshing your profile as you achieve more accomplishments

5. Not being proactive with "Recommendations"
Endorsements are a great way to build credibility. For example, your profile might show that Bob Smith and five other professionals endorse your social media skills. However, recommendations are more valuable because they require more than clicking a button. The most powerful ones are written by genuinely enthused people whose expectations you exceeded. Something to remember: a thoughtful and well-written recommendation from a peer who speaks with specifics can do more to distinguish your profile than generic comments from people who are many levels above you.

Solution: Take the time to personally invite each person to provide you with a recommendation, reminding them of your skills and what you did for them. Read the tutorial on how to ask for a recommendation on LinkedIn.

6. Not enough online Activity
While you want to keep a current and active profile, keep your LinkedIn activity relevant to your business sector, function, and discipline. The more you post - the higher your LinkedIn ranking. If you are a blogger, upload your posts and comment on other articles that have been posted. But remember – it's not Facebook. No one cares what restaurant you had dinner at last night or the cute picture of your dog or cat.

Solution: Use the 5-3-1 Formula on Page 28-29 to be a LinkedIn Power User.

7. Not Editing for Grammar and Typos

The worst thing that can happen is having a profile with poor grammar and typos. Have someone else look at your profile to notice any imperfections.

8. Not Creating a Personalized URL LinkedIn Profile Hyperlink

When you initially subscribe to LinkedIn, your profile link gets added with extra random (alpha-numeric) letters and numbers generated by the computer and added to your URL. It would be best if you personalize it with your name. If your name is not available, play with variations. For example, markjames444 or coachmarkjames. My LinkedIn profile is: **https://www.linkedin.com/in/markjamescpc/LinkedIn Demographics**

LinkedIn is a business-oriented social media networking site that enables users to connect with colleagues, look for a new job or business relationship, and get answers to industry questions. LinkedIn users can invite those they know and trust to become "linked in," and their business connections become your 2nd-degree connections. This is where the magic happens. Professionally ask your 1st-degree connection to provide an introduction on your behalf to one of their connections, your 2nd-degree connection. I refer to this as the **LinkedIn Shuffle** – it's like a "Two-Step" away from a formal introduction.

Still not convinced LinkedIn is suitable for you? Let's end this chapter with a few statistics:

1. LinkedIn now has over 900 million members and over 55 million registered companies in over 200 countries worldwide.
2. Of those LinkedIn users who frequently engage with the platform, 40% access it daily, clocking up over 1 billion monthly interactions. However, LinkedIn is used sparingly, so you only have a few minutes to make an impact. Users only spend about 17 minutes on LinkedIn per month.

3. According to the Pew Research Center 2018 Social Media Use study, LinkedIn remains popular with college students. Further research into these LinkedIn statistics revealed that 50% of college graduates in the US are LinkedIn users. In comparison, the site engages with only 9% of people whose education doesn't surpass high school.
4. Additionally, 44% of LinkedIn users take home more than $75,000 annually, above the US national median.
5. Although the US has the most LinkedIn users at 176 million, over 75% of LinkedIn users are from outside of the US.
6. Along gender lines, LinkedIn is more popular with men, who comprise 57% of its user base. Interestingly, millennials comprise over 60% of LinkedIn's user base, with 11 million of the 87 million millennials in decision-making positions.
7. Microsoft, recognizing the value of LinkedIn, acquired the company for $26.2 billion in 2016. However, unlike many other social media platforms that rely on advertisements, LinkedIn's services are something users are willing to pay for.
8. A total of 39% of LinkedIn users pay for LinkedIn Premium, which has four price tiers:

   ➢ Premium Career: $29.99/month
   ➢ Premium Business: $59.99/month
   ➢ Sales Navigator Pro: $79.99/month
   ➢ Recruiter Lite (Hiring): $119.95/month

Premium Career is best for those looking for jobs. It gives you access to 10 InMail messages per month and in-demand videos, as well as the ability to see who viewed your profile, how many searches you've appeared in, and additional information on posted jobs. The other tiers include essentially the same basic features but then go a step or two further.

Premium Business gives you additional information about businesses and unlimited people searches. **Sales Navigator Pro** gives you advanced search filters, access to different sales tools, and the ability to make user profile notes. **Recruiter Lite** gives you guided search-intelligent suggestions and more recruiter-focused tools. No matter which premium account you buy, you'll have access to improved metrics and various ways to achieve LinkedIn growth.

9. LinkedIn is an excellent source for discovering leads. HubSpot found that LinkedIn is 277% more effective at generating leads than Facebook and Twitter.

Phone Script: Call to a Recruiter who Viewed your LinkedIn Profile:

"Hello, My name is_____. I saw that you or someone from your firm visited my LinkedIn profile. Thank you. I know you recruit for companies that may need someone with my background and skills. Let's discuss your current job search assignment needs and how I might be a match.

I will send you a copy of my resume soon and follow up with you next week to answer any questions about my background and determine if there is a fit with any search projects you are currently working on. By the way, I have many talented contacts in my network and would happily provide referrals. My phone number is: _____ If I do not hear from you, I will call you next week to follow up.
Enjoy the day!"

Phone Script: Recruiter Cold Call

Hello,_____My name is_____. I'm reaching out to explore potential opportunities you may be working on for someone with my background and qualifications. I'm currently in [position] with [company] and am interested in exploring other positions. [If unemployed, you can say, "I have expertise and experience _____and am interested *in exploring positions where I can add value to a company in the__ _____industry.)*

May we schedule some time to discuss how I might be suitable for one of your clients?

The best number to reach me is_____. I will call you next week to follow up.

Enjoy the day!

You

Chapter 6

Contacting Executive Search Firms

Establishing a solid working relationship with any recruiter requires open and honest communication. If you are not interested in relocating to a new city, say so. If you are interested in a particular company, say so. If you are currently interviewing with one or several companies, say so. The one thing a recruiter is NOT interested in is wasting their time, their client's time, or your time. There are questions that a recruiter will ask to qualify you as a candidate for a particular opportunity, such as your salary requirements, relocation options, current position responsibilities, and current growth potential. Just as with answering questions for your doctor regarding your medical history, your answers will dictate the treatment you will receive. Given honest answers, your recruiter will know which opportunities and what companies would pique your interest, saving each of you time and energy and opening the door for you to find a better career opportunity.

Second, avoid the mistake of an actual recruiter with a resume factory. The differences are profound. A resume factory sends a stack of resumes to a company and sits back, waiting for the call that one of those resumes has produced a hire. In contrast, a professional executive recruiter is involved in the hiring process from the initial recruitment phone call through the entire interview process, the negotiation and acceptance of the offer, and concluding only with the start of employment with the client company.

A call from or made to a recruiter will not be a nuisance or an imposition when treated professionally and when the candidate is willing to follow these few simple ideas. The following is a list of things you can do as a candidate to assist an executive recruiter in making

them the most effective in managing your career:
- **LISTEN** – Learn something by opening your eyes and ears to the potential opportunity. At the very least, you will get off the phone with more knowledge regarding your industry, competitors, industry trends, what kind of companies are hiring, and your future career options.
- **ASK QUESTIONS** – How long have they been recruiting? What is their industry specialty? Are they Retained or Contingent? Do they work exclusively on search projects? What types of positions do they specialize in placing? *Are they listed in the Directory of Executive Recruiters?*
- **BE CANDID** – Time and honesty are essential elements in your world. Time is money. Honesty in dealing with a recruiter saves both parties time.
- **SHARE** – A candidate and recruiter relationship is one of give and take. The more open a candidate is with a recruiter, the more willing that recruiter will be to share details regarding potential opportunities in their field.
- **NAME NAMES** – When dealing with information, a recruiter values a candidate's willingness to refer friends and colleagues, which they greatly respect. If, as a candidate, you feel comfortable with a recruiter's professionalism, integrity, and approach, then you should be more than willing to refer an associate who might benefit from a call from that recruiter.
- **RESPOND** – During the interview phase, a recruiter offers valuable insight into the client company, the hiring authority, the interview process, and the post-interview activity. The key to a recruiter being effective in dealing with the client is the response they get from the candidate. Responses should be timely, complete, up-front, and sincere. *Don't play games with a recruiter – it won't work!*
- **DECIDE** – In any relationship, there comes a time when decisions

must be made. A candidate is best served when they can quickly evaluate the interview process and decide on the next step with the recruiter's help. Does the interview process need to continue? Are you ready to field an offer? What must the offer be to make the opportunity presented worth acting upon? All of these questions should be considered at each step and should be discussed openly with the recruiter.

Secrets Recruiters Don't Want You to Know

1. They only spend about 5-10 seconds looking at your resume and seldom read your cover letter unless they like it.

2. The salary could have gone higher - if you negotiated.

3. Time-worn embellishment buzz words and phrases are a major turnoff. For example, "What do you bring to the table?" "I am a Team Player or Change Agent."

4. You only get one chance to make a good impression.

5. You are rejected because your references were less than flattering.

6. The recruiter did a back-door reference check on you and found the truth.

7. The company promoted an internal employee, and the search ended.

8. Your last few social media posts were deal breakers. Watch out for your Digital Dirty Laundry.

9. If you are not asked for your job references, you are not in the running.

10. You are not the #1 candidate if the hiring process and final decision take longer than normal.

The Recruiter Mindset

11. You never hear back from the recruiter because you rambled too long about yourself and why you are so qualified.

12. You are rejected because you are anxious, needy, and desperate for a new job.

13. When asked for your reason for leaving or looking (The RFL), you reply, "Because you need to make more money." ***NEVER say this!***

Do's and Don'ts for Reaching Out and Following Up with Recruiters

DO: Immediately tell them the basics about you—who you are, where you work, and what you want to do next.

DO: (Once you've sent an email applying for a particular role) Be patient and wait five days before following up to see if you are being shortlisted. However, make sure you do follow-up, as each conversation is another opportunity to leave a good impression.

DO: Have someone proofread your email and resume for you. Don't rely solely on Spell Check. Although I like Grammarly.com a lot!

DO: Have a clear objective, request, or call to action. Don't beat around the bush. Let them know in your first email why you're reaching out to the recruiter and your primary goal for contacting them.

DO: If you get a rejection email, always follow up and ask for feedback. Offer to buy the recruiter a coffee (it's amazing what a $5 investment will get you) so you can meet and build a relationship.

DO: Use an AI writing tool like ChatGPT to help you write your email messages. But you shouldn't rely solely on it to compose a knockout customized email.

The Recruiter Mindset

DON'T: Be a stalker and leave multiple messages/emails per day. Don't be aggressive, needy, or belligerent. If you do – you risk getting blocked. Remember, you have no entitlement to a recruiter's time and help.

DON'T: Expect recruiters to drop everything to meet you face-to-face immediately. Accept that a 15-minute Zoom/Teams meeting is the norm nowadays.

DON'T: Send a long email. Keep it short and sweet, and show that you're genuinely interested. A great tip noted in the article: Add hyperlinks to provide more information without adding length. A generic email does nothing to differentiate how you're uniquely qualified for the job.

DON'T: Rehash what you already put in your resume. This is your opportunity to provide more info about yourself. Remember that the purpose of your email (when sent accompanying your resume) is to be even more specific than your resume.

DON'T: Never use salutations like Dear Sir/Madam OR To whom it May Concern. Too many job seekers send the same automated email to every recruiter or a generic one that could apply to anyone seeking that job. Always address the email person-to-person by first and last name.

DON'T: If your message is an obvious mass email, they'll spot it and be turned off. Never send one email blasting your resume to many recruiters. It makes you look anxious, needy, and desperate.

> *"Desperation is the world's worst cologne or perfume."*
> Mark James

The Recruiter Mindset

Chapter 7

When An Executive Recruiter Contacts You

Every recruiter has their favorite questions to screen candidates. Being ready and prepared to answer the following questions will increase your chances of being presented by an executive recruiter to their client company. Here are eight possible screening questions from a recruiter to anticipate and prepare your answers as the candidate.

The 8-Question Recruiter Interview

Question 1 – (Opening) Create an exciting position:
(Describe the overview of the company and position and significant objectives, then ask:)
Please give me a quick overview of how your background and experience have prepared you for this leadership position.

Question 2 – Determine the trend of personal accomplishments and energy:
(Ask this question for the past 2 – 3 jobs)
Please give me a quick overview of your (current/prior) position and describe the most significant impact (change) you made (or when you took the initiative).
(Spend 5-10 minutes fact-finding to understand the process used to achieve the results. Ask this same question for the past 2-3 positions to see the trend of personal accomplishments over time.)

Question 3 – Determine the trend of team leadership:
(Ask this question for the past 2 – 3 jobs)
Describe your organization (draw an organization chart) and tell me how you developed and managed your team (or tell me about some team project and describe your role. (Spend 5-10 minutes on fact-

finding. Ask this same question for the past 2-3 positions to see the trend of team leadership.)

Question 4 – Anchor* – Determine the comparability of past accomplishments:
(Ask for each **SMART*** objective.) One of our key performance objectives is _____ (describe objective). *Please tell me about your most similar past accomplishments.*

Question 5 –Visualization* – Determine the ability to adapt to and anticipate the needs of the position:
(Ask for just the top 2 objectives]
If you were to get this job, how would you implement and organize the _____ (describe performance objective)?
(Get into a give-and-take discussion with the candidate about real issues.)

Question 6 – Commitment, character, and values:
Tell me about a time you were committed to a task.
(Do fact-finding to understand better the actual accomplishment and how the candidate went the extra mile)

Question 7 – Personality and cultural fit:
What three or four adjectives best describe your personality? Give me examples of when these have aided in your job performance and when they have hurt. (Compare this personality to your 1st impression. Also, look for honesty and self-awareness.)

Question 8 – Create supply and express your interest in the candidate:
Although we see some other acceptable candidates, you have a solid background. We'll get back to you in a few days, but what are your thoughts now about this position? (Don't go too fast. Make the job worth earning. Create a competition to test genuine interest.)

The Recruiter Mindset

ANCHOR - From an employer's point of view, it should be essential to get a past comparable accomplishment to determine a candidate's ability to achieve a critical **SMART** objective.

SMART - **S**pecific, **M**easurable, **A**ction-oriented, **R**esult-based, **T**ime-bound
Example: "Within six months, improve factory production by 3%."

VISUALIZE—Determine the candidate's competency and ability to anticipate and understand the position's performance requirements. Well-prepared candidates should know their most significant **SMART** accomplishments ***and*** be able to relate **how** they would achieve their critical objective.

Quick Tips When Dealing with Recruiters
Good recruiters will be honest and communicative with you, but it helps to know their mindset when you reach out or meet with them.

1. Do your research. Google "Top Recruiters in your industry, function, and discipline. List 30-40 search firms to send your cover letter and resume.

2. Use your network for recruiter referrals and introductions.

3. Making a good first impression. Be friendly, and know how recruiters work.

4. Show an appropriate level of interest for the position.

5. Be prepared to discuss your resume and required cover letter, outlining your ideal company, salary requirements, job title, and approved job locations.

6. Say things that are easy to remember and repeat. Know your soundbites.

7. Be clear and concise. Provide relevant information in one message to

save time and avoid back-and-forth basic questions.

8. Be Honest. The relationship between and a candidate must have trust.

9. Be transparent. Be open and honest with applicants about the process.

10. Ask appropriate questions. Recruiters appreciate candidates voicing their opinions and doubts.

11. Follow their Advice and Feedback. Be responsive and respectful.

12. Build Relationships. Good connections can help recruiters get help figuring out their work processes.

> *"Past performance is a strong predictor of future performance. The candidate's ability to ANCHOR and VISUALIZE during an interview strongly predicts success."*
> Mark James

Chapter 8

The Interview Mindset

Job seekers often focus on what they seek in an ideal job (i.e., income, benefits, location, function, responsibilities, title, stature, drive time, industry, and corporate culture). On the other hand, hiring executives have an entirely different set of standards for what they seek in candidates. If you, as a job seeker, need to recognize the difference, you will be history in terms of being the candidate of choice. Let's explore the minds of decision-makers and find their hot buttons. When you search these factors through your resume and interviews, you are likelier to become the standard by which all other candidates will be measured.

Recruiter and Company Candidate Hot Buttons

1. Ability to do the Job. It sounds simple enough, but you would be amazed how many people apply for jobs for which they are not qualified. Before the decision makers dig deep into a candidate's background or invite them for an interview, they must confirm this fundamental criterion. Establish your ability through your resume or portfolio by emphasizing accomplishments, results in performance, and insights into emerging trends, opportunities, and challenges.

2. Initiative. Unless you are entry-level, most decision-makers seek someone who can "hit the ground running." They do not want a long learning curve that requires costly training and where the new hire cannot produce quick results. Today's decision-makers have very little patience. Demonstrate how you quickly identified a problem or need project, initiated an action plan, and produced bottom-line results.

3. Job Growth. Decision makers look for people beyond their defined "job description." Show that you are adaptive, willing to take on additional responsibility, and will go the extra mile to succeed. You don't want to be perceived as someone stuck in their comfort zone and always content with the status quo.

4. Self-Confidence. Decision makers want to know they can trust you to perform the job and produce the desired results. They develop this trust by seeing your confidence. Confidence can be displayed in numerous ways. Here are a few things decision-makers look for **A)** Speak with authority. Use phrases like "I can," "I will," and "I know." Avoid phrases like "I think," "In my opinion," and "I feel that." **B)** Demonstrate a commanding presence through your appearance, posture, eye contact, and body language. **C)** Show your track record of ongoing success. Decision-makers will not have confidence in you if they can only see a few accomplishments scattered over several years.

5. Leadership. Leadership is not reserved for senior executives or managers. For example, a janitor can show leadership by finding a better way to do their job, by setting an excellent example for their peers, or by finding ways to cut costs through more effective cleaning equipment or a new supplier for less expensive cleaning materials. Leadership is a rare commodity. Show decision-makers that you dare to take a leadership role, regardless of your level or function.

6. Compatibility. Much to the regret of some people, decision-makers look for a certain amount of conformity. Organizations and recruiters seek people whose personality style and behavior match the requirements of the job and the corporate culture. For example, we all know that the employee is never happy with anything, is a continual whiner, and always finds fault with everyone else. During your interviews, avoid criticizing your former employer or blaming others for why things didn't get done. Consistently demonstrate your (PMA) Positive Mental Attitude.

7. Attitude. OK, we wrapped up number six by mentioning your PMA.

Let's build on that. If you want to be the standard by which all others are measured, then walk in the door with a high energy level, tons of enthusiasm, a zest for living, and the determination to be the best at whatever you do. Enthusiasm is infectious. Others feed on it. It motivates and drives others to higher levels of productivity and success. Show your enthusiasm every chance you get, and you dramatically increase your chances of being hired.

8. Social Skills/Interests/Involvement. In today's business world, professional courtesy and conduct seem to be from another era. You can never say please and thank you enough. Give credit and praise to others. Discuss the team's performance and everyone else's contribution to your projects or job during your interview. Show interest in what others were working on and how you were willing to help. Show your involvement in organizational activities—both social and professional.

9. Integrity. Over the past few years, we have witnessed many of our nation's top senior-level executives' tragic abuse of authority and total lack of honesty, ethics, and integrity. During the interview, it is essential to demonstrate your uncompromising integrity, professional ethics, and personal morals. If a decision maker wants you to "wink" at laws or professional conduct, you don't want to work for that company.

10. Communication Skills. A good communicator possesses outstanding written and oral skills and knows how to use them effectively. Demonstrate to the decision maker how you continually use communication skills to achieve your goals. There is much information here, and hitting all these hot buttons through your resume and interviews is difficult. But by being aware of these hot buttons, you can consciously try to touch on as many as possible. Instead of what you want, focus on what the employer wants, and you will land that next job.

> ### The Five C's
>
> ### What Recruiters Look for:
>
> **Competence:** *Can you perform the job?*
>
> **Communication:** *Can you relate to people*
>
> **Compatibility:** *Can you do the requirements*
>
> **Chemistry:** *Can you do the job with the employees?*
>
> **Compensation:** *Can you do the job for what they will pay?*

3 Interview Preparation Tips

Here are some ideas for preparing yourself for what can come up in the first interview and training yourself to use each interview as an opportunity to improve your skills.

1. Ensure you understand why the job is a good fit and why you want it.

You will confidently respond to questions when you connect what you offer to what they need.

Can you identify your strengths? Do you know how disabling symptoms specifically impact your work and what you need to work around this?

You might want this job because it would improve your skills and be a good career move, even if it might be more challenging.

On the other hand, you might want this job because it would allow you to progress within a fast-growing, reputable company that recognizes its employees and rewards outstanding performance.

2. Job interviews are typically a series of events rather than a one-shot meeting.

Your goal in the first interview is to get to the next step.

Complete honesty is essential, but that doesn't mean you are telling your life story (such as you've been married three times) or disclosing chronic illness. An easy guideline is to say as much as you need to but no more than you have to.

If asked why you left your last job, which is pretty standard, the first interview is never the time to describe negative details, even if you left feeling resentment, bitterness, and anger at what you thought was poor treatment surrounding your termination and departure. Be prepared to give a positive "exit statement," i.e., the reason for leaving your previous job.

Note—the first interview is not the time to ask about the salary, benefits, and vacation time. Save those questions for later during the interview, such as when you receive a job offer. Asking them in the first interview may make you look desperate and not interested in the actual challenges and goals of the job.

3. View an interview as an opportunity to learn about the job and the organization.

This should be a two-way conversation in which you both try to determine whether this is the right fit and mutual benefit.

In addition, asking good, compelling questions in an interview is a sign to the interviewer that you have prepared, listened to, and thought about the job and the organization. Demonstrate your intelligence, and learn if the organization will be where you believe you can work happily and successfully.

The Six Interview Mindsets

Your leadership qualities will be scrutinized more closely in every interview than in previous recruitment processes. To shine, your attitude and mindset will be just as important as your technical and leadership competencies.

The logic is straightforward. If you don't demonstrate confidence in your ability to make a difference in a company, why should the "Decision Makers" (DM) have confidence in you? After all, they are making what will probably be their single most important decision - choosing the right person for the job. It's not unreasonable to expect they might be worried about making the wrong decision and be a little risk-averse.

As a short-listed or final candidate, you start with critical psychological advantages. First, congratulations; you are going to be presented by a recruiter. You have been narrowed down to many candidates, and your skills and competencies must align with the **Hiring Authority or Decision Maker (DM)**, the final decision-maker in the hiring process. You are already ahead of the game and have earned leverage.

Second, the DM desperately wants you to succeed at the interview. They start each interview by wanting the candidate to solve their problem and hire a new employee. In short, the decision-makers have got to believe that you are their next employee to be hired. This is where the right **Interview Mindset** is critical.

There is much more than having a mindset when you're in an interview. You have to have a plan. Please refer to the 23 interview questions with answer strategies in this chapter. You will need to develop stories about your accomplishments and examples. Get ready BEFORE you walk through the door for your interview at the company.

The Recruiter Mindset

Here are The Six Interview Mindsets:

Mindset #1 - The Doctor/Patient Mindset. When addressing an interview mindset, you pretend you play the doctor, and the hiring manager is the patient. When you are sick and visit the doctor, they ask questions to determine your condition so they can help. It's the same process during the interview. That's the doctor/patient mindset.

Mindset #2 - The Consulting Mindset. Act as a consultant. You're looking for problems that require solutions. What would you do differently in an interview if you had the mindset that you were acting as a consultant? You're trying to understand the issues and problems because that's what a consultant must do. They have to know how you will be able to help them. By the way, in that doctor/patient mindset, as you're determining whether or not they have problems, your question to them, as an interviewer, is, ***"What are the top five or six critical deliverables that the person that gets this job needs to do in the next six to twelve months?"***

It's the absolute number one question right out of the box when you get a chance. Then you're saying that this person needs to do that, needs to do this. You're not nominating yourself too soon because you don't know whether or not you want to do this job yet.

What if they give you menial types of responsibilities and goals that you used to do 10-15 years ago? Then that's going to be a challenging problem. You're not going to feel challenged on the job. You must determine what those deliverables are and if you're excellent at them. You're good to go with your examples and stories, and you can pull one of those examples out that matches up with one of the things that they bring up as one of the greatest deliverables or issues that they need to have this person solve in the next 6-12 months.

Mindset #3 - Pretend it's the First Day on the Job. You're thinking to yourself, "I've got this job. What am I going to do? How am I going to act?" You'll be confident, enthusiastic, and excited. You want to be in the moment, and you're going to go in there and try to figure out what the boss needs to be done. What's keeping him up at night? What are the significant objectives for the day, week, or month the boss completes? You're enthusiastic. Your mindset is different when you think of it going into an interview.

Mindset #4 - Be a Buyer - Not a Seller. I love this mindset. You don't know if you want this job yet. Don't sell too soon. Don't brag too quickly. Don't start crowing about your great examples and stories BEFORE you know what the Hiring Manager (HM) and company needs.

That's a big Sales 101 mistake. Where do you start doing a feature and benefits presentation before asking the customer what is needed?

You must know before you start delivering a solution, remedy, or answer to their problem. Buyer versus a seller. When you're a buyer, you ask compelling questions like "Why would somebody want to work here?" You don't know yet. You're not nominating yourself too soon. You're asking, "What must a person do to succeed?" Not "What do I need to do to be successful? Should you bring me on board?"

Don't nominate yourself too soon. Remember – be a **Human Switzerland and Stay Neutral.** There will be a time when you need to convert over and be committed to taking on this challenge, but you have to determine whether they can keep you motivated and if this will be challenging or boring.

Mindset #5 - Pretend You Won the Lotto. This mindset is fun: you drive home, pick up the groceries, and buy a lotto ticket, and you use that ticket as a prop to pretend that you've won the $500 million lotto. You remember that you're going into an interview tomorrow with the C.E.O. and the board chairman. You pick up the paper in the morning and realize that all your numbers match up and you've won millions of dollars. Do you still go on the interview, or do you not?

The Recruiter Mindset

What would your mindset be if you pretended you'd won the lotto and went on the interview? How would you act differently? What would you say? What would you do? You know there's nothing they can say to ruin your day because you've just won $500,000,000. You could buy the company if you were so inclined.

It's an exciting mindset because now you are more relaxed. You're more comfortable. You're going to be more likable. You might even have fun because you're learning about an opportunity, and what's going on in their company might be very exciting, but you might also think this isn't the right fit.

Try not to over-sell yourself and realize you didn't want the job. The key is not to allow the **Hiring Manager** to think you need the job more than the company needs you. Don't be aloof or act like you are not interested... keep in mind you have choices, too!

They may believe you are desperate, especially if you're out of work. They may think, "Well, jeez, we've got John in our back pocket if you need them more than they need you. We know he wants to work here. Bring in the next candidate to compare and contrast that person with John." But you're still evaluating the company if you give them the impression that you're not 100% on board. It's a two-way street. You've got to look at them as much as they look at you because these are critical decisions. These are business decisions, and you cannot afford to join the company for the wrong reasons.

Some statistics show that 50% of people take the first job offer that comes their way when they're out of work; 50% of the time, they're looking for a new job in six months because they jumped too soon. They ignored the red and yellow flags to get a paycheck. They settled for less, and now they're regretting it, and it's ten times worse now—maybe more.

Mindset #6 – Honesty + Ethics + Integrity. Along with projecting

Confidence and Enthusiasm during the job interview, you must address your reputation of possessing **Honesty, Ethics, and Integrity**, which can never be in short supply in business. A person's character often determines how successful they are in any career. A solid work ethic, remaining honest, and demanding self-integrity will be noticed on the job. Employers typically seek and promote workers that encompass these qualities. These three extraordinary characteristics must be the hallmark of your job interview narrative. When asked what your career strengths, skills, or competencies are – ALWAYS include Honesty, Ethics, and Integrity.

Honesty
Regardless of the job, honest behavior is crucial. Modifying a time card, filling out an expense report, allowing someone else to take the blame for your mistakes, or exaggerating circumstances on the job are all forms of dishonesty. Once an employer catches an employee or applicant in a lie, that employee may be fired or summarily dismissed from the hiring process. If the employee is not fired, that seed of doubt will be planted in the employer's mind. This may cause an employer to question the worker's honesty.

Ethics
In general, ethics are directly linked to moral principles. Ethics is the ability to tell the difference between right and wrong. Although an individual may know something is wrong, a good work ethic keeps him from taking that wrongful action. Work ethic is applying this principle on the job. Employees who exhibit a strong work ethic become a vital asset.

Integrity
Integrity can be described as the strength of someone's honesty and ethical standing. A person with solid integrity is less likely to be influenced by lesser moral values. Employers want to know that a worker will remain honest regardless of a co-worker's actions. Integrity reflects good moral character.

23 Tough Interview Questions with Answer Strategies

Here are some of my crucial interview questions. Try them out and hire a career coach or a friend to gauge your performance.

Pro Tip: Even if some of the following questions are not asked during your interview, you should find an appropriate time to share or insert your answers, philosophy, and beliefs into the *"give and take"* conversation.

1. Tell me about yourself.
Just talk for two minutes. Be logical. Start with college or your first job...OR ask, "Where would you like me to start?" The interviewer is looking for communication skills and linear thinking, so remember that seemingly innocuous questions such as "Tell me about yourself" are actually, "Why are you the ideal candidate for this position?" The best answers are honest, confident, and concise. Also, score a point or two by describing your primary attribute. **Hint: Use your Positioning Statement.** *(See pages 8, 9, and 10)*

2. Why are you leaving your current position or last job?
This is a very critical question. Don't "bad mouth" your previous employer. Don't sound "too opportunistic." It is best to relate major industry problems to a buy-out, shutdown, re-org, or downsizing. Also, it is good to state that after a long personal consideration, the chance to contribute is meager due to company changes. **Hint: Use your Exit Statement.** *(See page 7)*

3. What do you consider your most significant accomplishment?
This can get you the job. Prepare extensively. Score points. Tell a two-minute story with details and discuss personal involvement. Make the accomplishment worth achieving. Discuss hard work, long hours, pressure, and essential company issues at stake. Most importantly, tell them "HOW" you did it. You must create a value perception before the meeting has ended!

4. Why do you believe you are qualified for this position?

Pick two or three factors about you and your most relevant job. Discuss for two minutes with specific details. Select a technical skill, a specific management skill (organizing, staffing, planning, leadership), and a personal success attribute.

5. Have you ever accomplished something you didn't think you could?

The interviewer is trying to determine your goal orientation, work ethic, personal commitment, and integrity. Provide a good example of how you overcame numerous difficulties to succeed. Prove you're not a quitter and "that you'll get going when the going gets tough."

6. What do you like and dislike about your current and previous position?

The interviewer is trying to determine compatibility with the open position. If you are interested in the position, be careful. Stating that you dislike overtime or getting too deep into the weeds, like not agreeing with management, can cost you the position. There is nothing wrong with liking challenges, pressure situations, and opportunities to grow or disliking bureaucracy and frustrating situations.

7. How do you handle pressure situations? Do you like or dislike these situations?

High achievers tend to perform well in high-pressure situations. Conversely, the question could imply that the position is pressure-packed and out of control. Nothing is wrong with this as long as you know what you're getting into. If you perform well under stress, provide an excellent example with details giving an overview. Let the interviewer "feel" the stress by your description of it. **Use a "Philosophy + Real Life Example" answer approach.**

8. Give me an example of where you have demonstrated initiative.

The sign of a good employee is the ability to take the initiative. A proactive, results-oriented person doesn't have to be told what to do.

This is one of the significant attributes of success. Give short examples describing your self-motivation to convince the interviewer you possess this trait. Try to discuss at least one example in-depth. Your extra effort, strong work ethic, and creativity must be demonstrated.

9. What's your business career's worst or most embarrassing aspect?

How would you have done things differently now with 20/20 hindsight? This is a general question to learn how introspective you are and to see if you can learn from your mistakes. If you can, it indicates an open, more flexible personality. Don't be afraid to discuss your failures, mainly if you learned from them. This is a critical aspect of high-potential individuals.

10. How have you grown or changed over the past few years?

This requires thought. Maturation, increased technical skills, or increased self-confidence are essential for human development. To discuss this effectively is indicative of a well-balanced, intelligent individual. Overcoming personal obstacles or recognizing manageable weaknesses can make you an approachable and desirable employee.

11. Why would you hire you? (What are your most significant strengths?)

Be prepared. Know your Top 8 strengths and competencies. Create a passionate sentence for every strength. Select those attributes that are most compatible with the job opening. Most people say "management" or "good interpersonal skills" to answer this. Don't unless you can describe the specific characteristics of management (planning, organizing, results, hiring, staffing, recruiting, etc.) and/or how your relationship skills have proven critical to your success. Use the "**Bookend Answer**" approach. *(See page 63)*

12. What do you consider your most significant weaknesses?

Don't reveal deep character flaws. Instead, discuss tolerable faults that you are working towards improving. Show by specific examples how this has changed over time. Better still, show how a weakness can be turned into a strength. For example, concentrating on the details results in higher quality work even though it requires much overtime.

13. Deadlines, frustrations, difficult people, and silly rules can make a job difficult. How do you handle these types of situations?
Unfortunately, most companies face these types of problems daily. If you can't deal with petty frustrations, you'll be seen as a problem. You certainly can state your displeasure at the petty side of these issues, but how you overcome them is more important. Despite challenging circumstances, diplomacy, perseverance, and common sense often prevail. This is part of corporate America, and you must be able to deal with it regularly.

14. One of the biggest problems is _____. Can you describe your most comparable accomplishment? How would you implement this task or project?
Think on your feet. Ask questions to get details. Break it into sub-parts. You likely have some experience with the sub-sections. Answer these and summarize the total. State how you would go about solving the problem. Be specific. Show your organizational and analytical skills.

15. Give me an example of when you executed a project flawlessly.
The ability to get the job done, regardless of any obstacles, is a crucial trait of top performers. Failure to execute is one of the top reasons people fail. Be ready to describe another great story or example that demonstrates your competencies. **Tip:** Don't fall for the trick question. Nothing is "flawless." Just talk about a successful project.

16. Tell me about your biggest team-directed accomplishment in a difficult time or situation.
Top performers get the job done by utilizing the talents of others. No one can do it all. Top performers know this, and leading a team is something they are good at. Relating a solid example of your leadership skills is a strong predictor of future performance. **Tip:** Once again, watch

<u>out for the trick question.</u> Ignore "during a difficult time" – and talk about your biggest team-directed accomplishment.

17. How do you compare your technical skills to your management skills?

Many people tend to minimize their technical skills, either because they don't have any or they don't like getting into detail. Most successful managers possess good technical skills and get into enough detail to ensure they understand the information their group presents. Try a good balance here to be seriously considered for the position.

18. How has your technical ability been important in accomplishing results?

The interviewer believes he needs a strong level of technical competence and resourcefulness. Most strong managers have good technical backgrounds, even if they have avoided the details. Describe specific examples of your technical expertise and training, but don't be afraid to say you are not current. Also, you could give an example of how you resolved a technical issue by "accelerated research."

19. How would you handle a situation with tight deadlines, low employee morale, and inadequate resources?

If you pull this off effectively, it indicates you have strong management skills. Be creative. An example would be great. Relate your most arduous management task, even if it doesn't meet all the criteria. Most situations don't. Organizational skills, interpersonal skills, and handling pressure are critical elements of effective management. Good managers should be able to address each issue, even if they are not concurrent. Deftly handling the question is pretty indicative of your skills, too.

20. Are you satisfied with your career to date? What would you change if you could?

Be honest. The interviewer wants to know if they can keep you happy. Knowing if you're willing to make some sacrifices to get your career on the right track is essential. The degree of motivation is an important selection criterion.

21. What are your career goals? Where do you see yourself five years from now?

Most importantly, be realistic! Blue Sky stuff brands you as immature. However, there is nothing wrong with wanting a piece of the brass ring so you can comfortably retire. A reasonable goal is one or two management jumps in 3-5 years. If your track indicates you're in line for senior management in 10 years, it's okay to mention. **Hint: Use your Professional Objective Statement.** *(See pages 9 and 10)*

22. Why should we hire you for this position? What kind of contribution would you make?

This is an excellent chance to summarize. By now, you know the fundamental problems. Re-state and show how you would address it. Relate to specific attributes and specific accomplishments. Qualify responses with the need to gather information. Don't be cocky. Demonstrate a thoughtful, organized, strong effort kind of attitude.

23. How do you define success?

The best approach to answering this question is to reference specific examples of your successes and explain the factors that contributed to your achievements. Then, share how you applied what you learned from each experience to continue your professional development and generate positive results. Make sure that your definition of success requires a desirable talent that you possess, be it teamwork, empathy for others, self-motivation, or other valued soft skills. Make sure that your definition of success requires a desirable talent that you possess, be it teamwork, empathy for others, self-motivation, or other valued soft skills. This question can also be asked to the job interviewer.

The Bookend Answer Approach

This approach is an excellent way for you to frame your answer. When somebody says, "Why should we hire you for this job?" you say, "I believe you should hire me for this job because..." That's the front of the bookend; you deliver your content answer in the middle. Reflect on your top 8 competencies that you can frame sentences around, paying particular attention to the top three to five (out of 8) key attributes or characteristics that demonstrate your qualifications, strengths, abilities, and competencies. And when you finish that answer, you bookend it by saying, "That's why I believe you should hire me for this job."

The beautiful thing is that they hear it three times. They say it once, they listen to you say it once at the beginning of the bookend, and then they listen again at the end of your answer. And it's almost like a positive reinforcement type of thing.

Non-Verbal Communication

Fact: 93% of all communication is non-verbal. Listening, eye movement and contact, tone of voice, facial expressions, and body language reveal volumes during a job interview.

In the interview training session, I'm looking at their eyes, tone of voice, body language, facial expressions, etc. Neurolinguistic programming (NLP), which studies nonverbal communication, is critical to understanding. The best practitioners of NLP are HR managers, police detectives, lawyers, judges, doctors, and recruiters.

Certified NLP professionals have been trained to tell when somebody's making it up, telling the truth, or lying. It's in the eyes and the tone of their voice. Those things are reviewed, and I bring them up in case they're not making good eye contact and are tentative in the tone of their voice. If they end on a high note, I get concerned that they're uncomfortable answering. It's almost as if they're seeking approval, like asking, "Is that the right answer?" Whereas, if they end on a down note, it is much more authoritative, credible, believable, and understandable.

Zoom Job Interview Tips

When interviewing virtually, there are some things you should do—and things you shouldn't—if you want to make the best impression. Companies are shifting from in-person to remote interviews, so conducting interviews via video call is essential. In a recent survey of talent leaders and recruiters, 80% of respondents said their hiring process is entirely remote. In comparison, 39% have increased their video conferencing software, like Zoom, for the interview process.

That's good news if you are looking for work because you can interview for jobs from the comfort of your home. However, virtual interviewing comes with challenges, mainly if you're not used to meeting remotely. It's too easy to get flustered by the technology and forget the details that make the difference between a so-so interview and one that clinches a job offer. Increase your chances of making a good impression and getting the job. There are inevitable mistakes you should avoid before and during Zoom interviews:

1. Arrive Early to the Online Interview

When it comes to job interviews, if you're not early, you're late. Being late for a tee time or doctor's appointment is never okay, and it's even more critical for Zoom interviews. Jump on the call a few minutes early, and you won't have to worry about last-minute technical difficulties derailing your effort. There's nothing worse than starting a job interview stressed out and distracted. Always confirm your interview details before your meeting day to ensure you're on time and prepared.

2. Practice with the Technology Beforehand

Speaking of technical difficulties, you can avoid many of them by making sure you're comfortable with the software ahead of time. Be sure to download Zoom and attend at least one practice interview before the event. You'll feel more at ease during the conversation and more resilient if other technical issues arise.

3. Gather Your Documents and Materials
Once you're seated in front of your computer, you should be able to reach everything you need to carry out a successful interview. Ensure you have all your interview materials, i.e., your resume, references, portfolio, etc., and that you're comfortable and ready to speak.

Although you shouldn't eat or drink during the conversation, you should have a glass of water ready in an emergency. (Interview nerves can cause dry mouth, so it's better to take a sip of water than to cough your way through the meeting.)

4. Dress to Impress
"An ounce of image is worth a pound of performance." If you are accustomed to being at home in sweats or pajamas for an extended period, it might be hard to remember the appropriate professional attire. Business attire or casual attire is usually the best bet for job interviews. A pressed shirt, sportscoat, dark-colored dress, nice top, blazer, or sweater are safe bets. Try to match your outfit to the company's culture as you understand it. Find out in advance what the dress code is and go one level up, even if employees keep it casual.

Remember that whatever you choose should look professional and show well on camera. Avoid stripes, extremely bright colors, or clothing in the same shade as your background. Even if the interviewer can't see the lower half of your body, it's a good idea to wear appropriate attire. You'll conduct yourself more professionally and avoid showing off your pajama pants if you need to stand up for some reason.

5. Present a Professional Background with Good Lighting
Zoom allows you to choose a default background image or upload your professional headshot photo. Make sure the lighting in the room is

adequate. Buy an inexpensive light ring with a tripod to plug into an open USB port in your computer or laptop. Clean up and organize your room to present a professional experience if you don't use a virtual background. Why? Research shows that your work environment affects your mental health and decision-making ability. In short, a quiet workspace promotes peace of mind.

6. Avoid Distracting Habits

Perhaps the worst Zoom interview mistake is to indicate that you're not interested in what the interviewer says through your behavior and mannerisms. Unfortunately, this is easier to do than you might think. Little gestures can make a significant impact. Fidgeting with your hair or clothes, checking your phone (yes, even off-screen), or staring at yourself instead of connecting with the interviewer can make it seem disconnected or distracted.

7. Carry on a Real Conversation

Some job interviews can feel like interrogations, even face-to-face. Video technology can exacerbate this problem by shrinking your visual field to two screens and ratcheting up the tension with the threat of technical difficulties. To overcome these issues, remember that a good job interview is a conversation—no more and no less. You and the interviewer are not on opposing sides but on the same team, working toward a common goal. Focus on listening instead of waiting for your chance to speak. You'll demonstrate valuable soft skills (EQ), communicate better, and learn more about the job. Best of all, you'll make a more favorable impression on the hiring manager, essential to helping you land the job.

8. Make the Best Impression

Practice makes perfect: This may not always be the case, but if you take the time to ensure you prepare and your technology is working correctly, the interview will be much less stressful. Get set ahead: Don't wait until the last minute to set up your interview space, clear away the clutter, and get your interview clothes ready. Remember to pay attention. It can be hard when interviewing remotely, so remember to listen carefully to the questions and focus on your interviewer.

> *"Don't love something that may not love you back."*
> Mark James

The Recruiter Mindset

Chapter 9

Closing the Deal: Salary Negotiation

Congratulations! After a long and arduous job search, you get a job offer. But how do you know if it's a good one?

In this chapter, I will review the main aspects you should evaluate when assessing any job offer and provide worksheets to evaluate job offers.

Accepting a job can be a big decision, and evaluating a job offer isn't easy. It's crucial to understand how to evaluate a job offer before deciding whether you can negotiate for something better.

There is an old saying, **"Don't love something that does not love you back."** Evaluating a job offer is not simple and should be done carefully. Statistically, your leverage to tailor your job description, increase your salary, and improve your benefits is more vital at the job offer stage than at any point. Now is the ultimate time to negotiate, close all loose ends, and get the offer the way you want. Assess the offer based on your needs. Hopefully, you have researched whether the offer is competitive and fair based on your city and state, cost of living, commute distance, etc.

Besides the headliner metrics like salary, job title, and responsibilities, you should also consider aspects contributing to your happiness and job satisfaction. There is no perfect job offer – but with an honest assessment and negotiating the exemplary aspects, you can tweak any job offer to suit your needs better.

How to Assess a Job Offer

1. Salary plus Bonus and Incentives

Consider all compensation. Even when you think the offered salary is adequate, does the market rate consider your qualifications? Compensation packages these days are often multifaceted—base salary, bonus/incentive packages, profit sharing, retirement, and benefits all contribute to the monetary aspect of any job offer.

What is the market rate? Continually benchmark the compensation of a job offer to know where you stand. Databases like Glassdoor, Salary.com, and Payscale.com are good starting points to find more salary data. Don't just check one website – check them and compare your research notes.

Negotiation: If you plan to negotiate on salary, have a strong reason (or set of causes) why you should be offered a higher package. It would help if you also had a backup plan – assess other aspects of the job, such as an early salary review based on your above-average performance. You can also ask for a percentage (50%) of your first year's bonus guaranteed during your new job assimilation ramp-up period.

2. Opportunities for Growth

Would you prefer to be leading a big team, with a few people or none at all? There are several aspects to this, and you must assess them honestly:

- ✓ **Training and Development:** Do you deserve more responsibility based on your previous role?
- ✓ **Autonomy:** Do you want opportunities for promotion, added management responsibilities, and more freedom and independence to make decisions?
- ✓ **Individual Contributor:** Do you naturally enjoy managing and interacting with people, or do you prefer a role as an individual

contributor?

- ✓ **Travel requirements.** What degree of traveling would the job require? Does that fit into your current life and family obligations? Will this allow you to have a 50/50 work-life balance?
- ✓ **Team interaction.** Depending on your personality, do you prefer to work in large teams, smaller teams, or with as few people as possible?
- ✓ **Client-facing time:** Do you want to be client-facing to develop your relationship management skills and improve your professional network, or would you instead free up valuable time to focus on developing your core professional skills?

3. **Leadership Development**

Skill development. While you'll almost always learn something new in any role, consider whether the development opportunities align with your long-term plans. For example, suppose you have extensive experience and skills in research and want to spend more time developing your presentation and communication skills. In that case, you might prefer a role with more opportunities to face internal or external clients.

Long-term goals. Is the job pointing you in the right direction for your long-term career? If you want to build management skills, you might choose a role with team members reporting to you, even if the other positions offer better perks or better pay. Seek to be challenged and utilize your full capabilities.

4. **Cultural Fit**

Ask yourself, *"Will I be happy and enjoy working here?"* It's challenging to know for sure without actually spending proper time there. Reach out to your contacts and LinkedIn network to get a better idea. Ask them about their firm's opinion, how long people tend to stay, or what happened to the last person who did the job. Glassdoor also provides comprehensive employee reviews of their workplace culture for larger companies.

5. Quality of Life

Vacation, Paid Time Off, and Remote Work Flexibility. Vacation time and the ability to work flexible hours are increasingly valuable perks. If flexible work hours are high on your priority list and not explicitly given in your work contract, raising this in the negotiation stage is a good idea. Most companies are flexible about allowing remote work and telecommuting. Negotiate to work remotely from home two or three days each week to avoid long, time-wasting commutes. Research bicycle paths, train access corridors, subways, carpooling, or other travel-related benefits that match your commuting plan.

6. Your Manager and Co-Workers

One of the most critical "happiness and unhappiness factors" at work relates to working with your boss and co-workers. Here's something they'll probably never teach you in business school. The most significant decisions you make in your job – more prominent than the rest – are those you report to and work arm-to-arm. People quit their jobs primarily because of personality conflict, unsatisfying management relationships, and poor communication.

Setting the Stage to Negotiate by Email

First, congratulations. You've received an offer! The more difficult news is that the job search process isn't over. It's time to consider the offer, compare it with your other options, and, most importantly, negotiate.

If you've just received a job offer, especially over email, crafting a quick message is a way to strike while the iron is hot for salary negotiation. The best approach is to keep your salary negotiation emails polite, professional, and direct. You want to demonstrate that you are thoughtful and organized and respect your supervisor's time. Be thankful for the opportunity you've been given, and avoid being pushy or entitled.

As to the specifics – here's how to respond to the offer you've received:

Step 1: Thank the employer for the offer
The hiring manager must know you're excited and grateful to accept this offer. The most appropriate language in this email is phrases about working together. You are excited about working together at this company and looking forward to finding a salary and benefits package suitable for both of you. You can even restate the offer in their terms, using a sentence like, "I am very grateful for your offer of [salary], but..."

Step 2: State your counter-offer
The number you state in the email is the jumping-off point for negotiations and not necessarily the number you expect will ultimately be offered to you. Utilize a tone that is respectful, polite, and professional. It's also important to remember that most employers expect a counteroffer and have wiggle room for most first job offers. Test drive a few phrases (below) to see what works best. Here are some effective phrases and some to avoid:

Effective Phrases
"Based on my previous compensation package, my goal is to be whole."

"Do you mind if I ask you the salary range for this role?"

"Can we discuss the other components of the compensation plan?"

"How willing are you to… [insert negotiable point or item?]"

Ineffective Phrases
"I will not accept anything less than X."

"I need a higher salary to pay my bills."

Step 3: Back Yourself Up

The salary number you ask for doesn't mean much if you can't back it up with research and justification. Research is one of the most important things you can do to make your salary negotiation successful. Always cite your sources, primarily if you rely on numerical information to support your question.

Candidates often forget to explain why they want or deserve a higher salary. Researchers have found that negotiators who include why they deserve something are 20% more effective than those who don't.

Remember: The company needs to make you an offer to evaluate first. Don't negotiate against yourself. Know the salary range for the position before you proceed. Use the illustration on the next page to plug in your numbers. This will help you set the stage to optimize your best possible offer based on the position **grade level or salary range.**

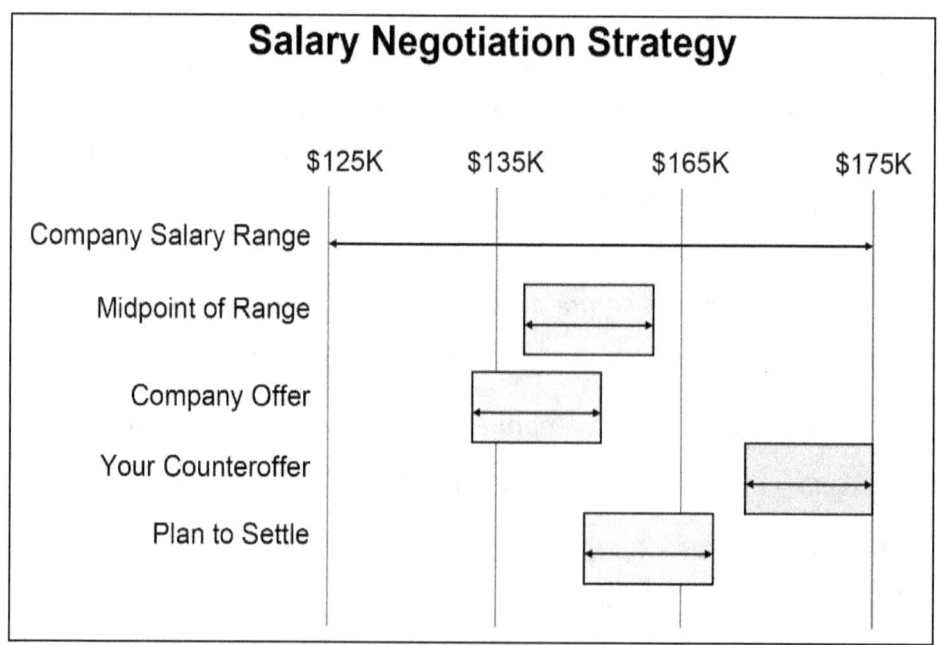

The Recruiter Mindset

Negotiating Statements About Your Salary Requirements

(Not including search firms) Your (demands=requirements) responses could be any of or a combination of the following:

• *"I think salary is a vital topic, and I would be more than happy to discuss it once a mutual interest has been established."* (Get back to discussing your accomplishments)

• *"Your company has an excellent reputation, and I'm sure the compensation package will be fair enough to keep me motivated and productive. By the way, what is the salary range for this position?"*

• *"Based on my accomplishments and contributions, I expect to be paid the same level as other executives of my tenure and caliber."* Then, ask, *"What is the salary range for someone of my caliber?"*

• *"Regarding compensation, I am flexible and willing to negotiate once we have developed a mutual interest."* (Get back to discussing your accomplishments)

• *"If we decide that I am the right person for this job, I am sure we will be able to agree on compensation."* (Get back to discussing your accomplishments)

• *"At this time, I am most interested in determining if I am the right person for this job. If there's a fit, I'm sure salary won't be an issue."* (Get back to discussing your accomplishments)

• *"Are you making me an offer? If so, what salary range did you have in mind?"* (Only use this response later in the process)

Know your Numbers in advance:

- ✓ What do you <u>really</u> NEED?
- ✓ What do you <u>really</u> WANT?
- ✓ Everything is Negotiable

Second Round Negotiations

NOTE: Conduct the 2nd Round of Negotiations in person - if possible. Go back to the Hiring Manager (not Human Resources) and say:

- *"This is a great opportunity, and I am excited about working with you* (or) *joining your company."*

- *"I am inclined to accept your offer; however, there are 3 (or more) items I want to discuss (negotiate) with you."*

- *"If we can agree on these items, I will be prepared to accept your offer today."*

Your Attitude and Assumptions

Your Attitude and Assumptions will determine 80% of the Outcome of Your Salary Negotiations!

Now, Set the Stage for Negotiation - Here's Exactly What to Write in your follow-up email.

Here is an email template to serve as the primer discussion for your salary negotiation email. This template is ideal because it's brief and to the point, fits the needs of busy hiring managers and recruiters, and is polite, clear, and direct.

Dear **[Name of Hiring Manager]**,

Thank you for offering me the position. I am excited about the opportunity and can't wait to start.

I want to discuss the following items on our scheduled call:

1. **Guaranteed base salary**
2. **Bonus/Incentive % breakdown**
3. **Profit-Sharing/Stock Options/RSU's**
4. **Sign-on bonus**

5. Early performance/salary review
6. Vacation weeks/PTO

Remember, this will help prepare the Hiring Manager to be ready to discuss each item you have listed. This is a jumping-off point, and further negotiations may come later. Asking to discuss the offer in brief terms will help you optimize your salary package and get what you are worth.

Keep Calm and Close the Deal

"My ultimate goals are to be the best person you ever hired, make your job easier, and be proud that you selected me for this role."

Negotiate the Optimum Salary Package

For years, I have coached hundreds of executives through successful negotiations, like the dialogue examples below. To make it even easier, I've broken it down into four easy-to-follow steps.

Step One: Try to Delay the Salary Topic

Note: In some states, like California, asking about your prior salary history is illegal. But, if you are asked what your salary requirements are by an HR Manager or Hiring Manager (HM), try to delay the conversation until the offer is made. If they ask you your salary requirements during the interview or on a phone screen, say something like this:

"My number one priority now is to learn more about your organization and this role to determine if I'm the best match for your needs. Should an offer be extended, I'd be happy to negotiate with you at that time, and I'm confident we'll reach an agreement."

This usually distracts the conversation from salary. However, if they insist on discussing it at that point, ask them to disclose the company's range first.

Step Two: Find the Salary Range for Your Role

Why find the range? You don't want to offer something too high and make the employer think they can't afford you. On the other hand, you don't want to offer something too low and miss out on a larger paycheck for yourself.

It's best to handle this by saying something along these lines:

"I'd be happy to negotiate with you. First, I'd like to know what the company has budgeted so I can negotiate within that range. What salary range is the company looking at?"

Saying this will ensure you can make a fair offer to both parties.

Step Three: Make a Ranged Offer

When you disclose your offer, always give them a range, not a specific number. Come prepared with a range of quotes. That range should be something you know is realistic for that position and that you would be comfortable accepting if they offered you. You can find salary range information based on location, title, and industry on these online websites: Glassdoor.com, Payscale.com, and Salary.com.

Step Four: Know Your Comfort Zone

Always have your ideal number and "deal-breaker" number you will not accept. When you are receiving a position that pays less than you currently make, you can handle this by saying:

"Compensation is important, but it's not my only priority. I'm more concerned about finding a position I can enjoy and grow in. If an offer is extended, we can reach a fair agreement on a salary that works for both parties."

This helps keep the dialogue open when it comes time to negotiate fully.

Executive Negotiating Statements

What do you say when asked for your salary requirements? Remember, the company needs to make an offer for you to evaluate it—not the other way around! Know your numbers in advance. Determine what you really need and what you really want.

Your (demands=requirements) responses could be any of or a combination of the following:

- *"I think salary is a very important topic, and I would be more than happy to discuss it once a mutual interest has been established."* (Get back to discussing your accomplishments)
- *"Your company has a very good reputation, and the compensation package will be fair enough to keep me motivated and productive. By the way, what is the base salary range for this position?"*
- *"Based on my accomplishments and contributions, I would like to be paid at the same level as other executives of my tenure and caliber."* And ask, *"What is the salary range for a person of my caliber?"*
- *"Regarding compensation, I am flexible and willing to negotiate once we have developed a mutual interest."* (Get back to discussing your accomplishments)
- *"If we decide that I am the right person for this job, I am sure we will be able to agree on compensation."* (Get back to discussing your accomplishments)
- *"At this time, I am most interested in determining if I am the right person for this job. If there's a fit, I'm sure salary won't be an issue."* (Get back to discussing your accomplishments)
- *"Are you making me an offer? If so, what salary range did you have in mind?"* Only use this response later in the process.

Second and Final Round Negotiations

Go back to the Hiring Manager (not Human Resources) and say:

- *"This is a great opportunity, and I am excited about working with you (or) joining your company."

- "I am inclined to accept your offer; however, there are 3 (or more) items I want to discuss (negotiate) with you."

- "If we can agree on these items, I will be prepared to accept your offer today." Remember, if you ask for and receive something, you must give something in return. That's how deals are made.

- Always try to conduct this negotiation "in person" if possible!

- 80% of the outcome of your salary negotiations will be determined by your optimistic attitude and accurate assumptions!

- Remember, everything is negotiable, and get everything in writing!

Job Offer Checklist *(Don't leave anything on the table.)*

1. Job Title
2. Position reports to
3. Start Date
4. Salary (monthly or bi-monthly pay periods)
5. Performance Review Date
   - 6-month early review?
6. Commission structure
7. Bonus
   - Eligibility? % Company Performance vs. Individual Performance
   - Is it possible to get a pro-rate bonus during the first year?
   - Guarantee a portion of the first year's bonus
8. Signing bonus
   - Verbally indicate to compensate for lost bonus/stock options, etc.
9. Vacation weeks /Paid Time off / Maternity leave

- Extra weeks rather than a higher base?
- Working Remotely and Telecommuting

10. Health Insurance
    - Effective date
    - Monthly Premiums/Co-Pay/Annual deductible

11. Retirement: Matching 401K

12. Stock options, Profit Sharing, Equity

13. Company Car or Monthly Allowance

14. Travel and entertainment expenses

15. Club membership

16. Executive Coaching

17. Relocation Expenses
    - Temporary housing
    - # of trips home
    - House hunting trip(s) with spouse
    - Real estate fees
        a) selling end - pickup 5% - 7% commission? Points?
        b) buying end - closing costs
    - Packing & moving household goods
    - Discretionary amount for miscellaneous expenses
    - Gross-up taxes

18. Trailing Spouse Career Transition Coaching Assistance

19. Separation/termination Agreement
    - 6-12 months full salary and family health benefits

20. Employment Offer/Acceptance Contingencies
    - Drug Tests/Physical Exams/ Behavior Assessments
    - Verification of college degree

- Employment References and Background Check
- Financial Credit checks

21. Offer Letter reviewed by an employment attorney

5 Salary Negotiation Tips that Work!

Once you've proven yourself well-qualified for a job during the interview process, you must ask yourself the tough questions. Do you have a strong desire to work for this company? What if they don't offer as much money as you'd like? Is there a way to ask for a higher salary without alienating the employer?

It's normal to feel anxious or nervous. But you can learn practical negotiating skills that will help you get what you want, need, and deserve in terms of compensation.

1. Understand Benchmarking

You don't want to waste your valuable time on a company that will never pay you what you're worth. You must understand how employers decide their salary levels and adjust your job search accordingly. Companies use a variety of benchmarking tools. These include comparing pay rates with:

- Average pay at other companies in their industry
- Average pay for professionals with your level of experience and education
- Average pay for professionals in your field in their area of the country

Most employers who are interested in great talent will be in the upper quartile of their market when it comes to salary. However, employers have also figured out that paying significantly more than their competitors doesn't motivate employees to stay over the long term. So, don't expect to be able to negotiate for substantially higher pay than the norm – no matter how qualified you are.

2. Wait for It…

There's an old saying, "The first person to bring up money loses." Starting a discussion about salary prematurely signals that you don't prioritize being a good fit for a company's culture – you care about the almighty dollar. In the same way, if a recruiter brings up money right off the bat, it's a good idea to change the subject so you can fully demonstrate your qualifications before talking about your salary requirements.

3. Negotiate Performance Pay

An employer who really wants to hire you but has limited resources may offer a lowball figure with the excuse, "This is what we can afford right now." If you want the job, ask if they would be open to discussing a performance-based bonus. You could start by saying, "Let's discuss specific, measurable results that would improve your bottom line and increase my earnings." Get any incentive pay agreements in writing during the hiring stage so your employer is committed to following through.

4. Don't Just Talk Cash

Any discussion of salary should be about your total compensation. If the recruiter isn't familiar with the dollar value of the company's benefits package, you might ask to talk with their benefits specialist. Remember to negotiate for non-cash perks that might bridge the gap between your asking price and the employer's offer.

5. Walkthrough It in Training

One of the best ways to prepare is by practicing. Pick a career coach who can prep you by role-playing an entire interview, including the salary negotiation phase. This process gives you the confidence to talk money with a potential employer without fear of getting it wrong.

> **"L.U.C.K. =
> Learning Utilizing Correct
> Knowledge"**
> Mark James

Chapter 10

Offer Acceptance, Job Resignation, and Counteroffers

Before you say "Yes" and accept a job offer, know these:
Your particular needs for choosing the right company. What are your passions? What are the lessons that you've learned? What are your accomplishments, which are story examples, and what are your needs? What are your needs? The needs are people, challenge, balance, and worth. Those are the four criteria to rank to determine whether or not this is the right company for you to go to work with, accept their job offer, and join that company.

People are important. That always has to be number one. You have to like them. They have to like you. You have to be able to learn from them. They have to be able to learn from you. You want to be inspired by these people. You want to know they've got vision. They're all on board. If you're the sharpest arrow in the quiver, it will be a long, long ride. You will not like it very well if you're the sharpest arrow in the quiver or the sharpest needle in the quill, and they're all looking up to you for the answers, and you're around many people who are just lost. You will not like that job and will look for a new one in six months or less. There is also no chance for you to grow there.

I always say it's got to be the most challenging type of opportunity for you to want to get out of bed in the morning because your bank account does not get you out of bed. Your balance in your checking account does not get you to hit the snooze alarm. It's the motivation. It's the challenge, the charge, the "can't wait to do this and make a difference in the world," that you got to love what you're doing to get out of bed in the morning.

Money is a stimulator. Not a motivator. This is a fact. They do not motivate people to accept and go to work when offers are made. The money is put on the table to stimulate them to accept it. Then, the negotiation is a whole different thing, but people challenge and then balance. Balance is work-life balance. There is no mystery here. Some people want to work to live. Some people live to work. Know this before you say yes.

Does your plan sit well with the company? Some companies expect 70 hours a week, like a New York law firm, and others want you to go home after 40 hours. Suppose you're a soccer Saturday mom or dad, and you've got to be up and taking kids to soccer games or picking them up after school. In that case, your work-life balance is different from the guy who's an empty nester or the lady, the mom, who's no longer managing a family, where they can jump on a plane tomorrow morning to Albany, New York and be happy doing it without causing trauma in the family.

Work-life balance is an essential state of affairs, and you need to know it before saying yes. That changes as we all mature and grow older, and our kids grow up and raise their own families. Ask yourself, "Is it going to be disruptive in your life?" Are you going to be able to embrace the company and do what they need you to do?

Some statistics show that 50% of the unemployed people who take the first job offer that comes their way end up looking for a new job in six months because they jumped too soon. They ignored the red and yellow flags because they wanted to get back in the ranks and on the payroll. They did not play the field and jumped way too soon. They settled for less money and a lower job title, and now they regret it. The key decision-making criteria are **People + Challenge + Balance** *(work vs. life)* **and Worth.**

The Recruiter Mindset

Here are the Top 4 Criteria to Make the Right Decision Every Time:

1. **PEOPLE** – When deciding to work for a new company, it is all about the people! You want to like them and be liked. The People Likeability Factor" goes both ways, and it is the absolute most essential criterion in your decision to accept a job offer. You want to be appreciated and inspired by your fellow employees and company leaders. Good people chemistry, cultural fit, and cooperative personalities are the key ingredients that make work fun. Beware: You don't want to be the most intelligent person on the team. It would be best if visionary people around you inspired you. Being the sharpest arrow in the quiver will get old and boring. One of your primary reasons for joining a new company should be to learn and expand your knowledge through your talented co-workers. This is accomplished by working with highly skilled and intelligent people who work well together and synergize with each other's strengths.

2. **CHALLENGE** – The work you will be doing in your new job must be challenging, or you will get bored quickly and find yourself climbing the walls. The "Role Challenge Factor" must be evident, or you will eventually be looking for a new job again in 6 months or less. To avoid choosing the wrong position and role in an organization, never settle for less responsibility than you can handle and always be thinking about the next level of increased management responsibilities. Does the new job opportunity include advancement as a reward for your above-average performance? If not, you risk not being challenged or inspired to deliver your best effort. It is best if you are motivated to make a difference to achieve the company's objectives and vision.

3. **BALANCE** – The "Work and Life Balance Factor" is essential because we do not live to work -- we work to live! A person who works 60-80 hours a week will not have much life to enjoy the

fruits of their labor. Remember that each person's lifestyle changes as they progress during their career. Their children grow up, go away to school, move out, and start lives and families of their own. Being a "Soccer Saturday" Dad or Mom is no longer a parent requirement. At that point in your life, you have more freedom and flexibility to jump on a plane and travel out of town on business immediately. Your time dedicated to the job is only relative to the current obligations to your family and friends.

4. **WORTH** – As in Salary. Will the company be able to pay you what you are worth in the form of annual salary (guaranteed cash compensation) plus incentives and stock options, etc., based on your "Worth Contribution Factor" to the new company? Remember, it's not all about money because **"Money is not a Motivator – it is a Stimulator!"** When a company decides they need you, they will have to induce (stimulate) you to accept their good faith offer of employment. Your compensation goal is always to remain whole and never settle for less. Do your homework to research management-level pay scales to determine industry, function, and discipline competitiveness with similar companies.

The secret to using these four criteria is to rank each of the Top 4 Criteria on a scale of 1-10 (10 = ideal or best) to determine if your current job opportunity meets your essential needs and requirements. Anything criteria ranked less than seven is suspect and should not be ignored. Hint: These four criteria rankings should be used as your **"Negotiation Factors"** to make the right decision every time.

Then, the final criteria (worth) will always be whether a company can afford to pay you what you're worth based on your contribution. Rank the People, Challenge, Balance, and Worth on a scale of 1-10. (10=ideal) Anything less than 7 is suspect.

The Recruiter Mindset

The 5 things everyone wants from their job, but you can only get 3 consistently.

Here are five criteria for job happiness. The catch is that you will probably only be able to achieve 3 of these consistently in your "ideal" job. Which three are the most important to you? Which 2 are you willing to sacrifice?

1. Live where you work
2. Love whom you work with
3. Love what you do
4. Work reasonable hours
5. Make good money

Criteria Notes:

1. Are you willing to get on a plane every week, week in and week out, to do what you love? Do you hate to commute but are okay with being on an airplane to travel for work? Then you don't need to live where you work vs. someone who hates driving for 1 hour to work for a job.

2 and 3. "Love" is intentional in these two criteria. Not like, not enjoy, but love.

4. "Reasonable hours" is how you define it. 60+ hours per week may be reasonable if you love what you do.

5. "Good money" is how you define it. You may work for the Forestry Service, earn $100K annually, and think you're overpaid. Or you may work on Wall Street and earn $1M per year, and it's never enough.

Resignation Assitance

Congratulations! You have received and accepted an offer of employment and are ready to take the next step in advancing your career. While you must be very excited about the opportunity ahead, you must also think about how to leave your current position.

The Recruiter Mindset

Many people about to resign from their jobs feel somewhat apprehensive about it. As they say, "Breaking up is hard to do." You have worked hard for your current employer and are a valued employee. You probably have made lots of friends and have people who count on you. Telling these people you are leaving can be difficult. As you get ready to resign, it is essential to remember that you are not rejecting the people you work with. Instead, you are deciding to advance your career.

Be sure to stay in contact with your recruiter throughout the process. They can help you tailor this to your situation if necessary. Good luck!

Preparing to Resign

The key to resigning gracefully and professionally is to keep control of the discussion and focus on the great opportunity ahead of you. Here are some thoughts that will help you prepare:

- Ensure you have a signed offer letter from your new employer.
- Set an appointment to meet with your boss in person (or over the phone, if necessary) on the day you plan to resign.
- Write your resignation letter. You can adapt the attached template to suit your needs.
- Plan what you will say when you meet with your boss. Your resignation letter can serve as a script.
- Important points to include both in your letter and at your meeting:
    - Express appreciation for the opportunity to work with the company
    - State that you have accepted and <u>committed</u> to another position
    - State the effective date of your resignation (you should give two weeks' notice)

- Give a brief description of what you will be doing in your new position
- State what you will do to ensure a smooth transition
- Remind them what they owe you in unpaid bonuses, commissions, unreimbursed expenses, unused vacation or sick days, etc.

Controlling the Discussion

Be clear and definitive about your resignation. Stick to the script you prepared, keeping the discussion brief and positive. Don't burn any bridges. Never say anything negative about the company, your position, or the people you work with. Instead, let them know you are leaving because a career-enhancing opportunity came your way that you couldn't pass up.

Avoid answering questions about why you are leaving. This will make the discussion too negative and could cause you to lose control. One way to deflect these questions is to focus the debate on the opportunity ahead of you and to restate your commitment to this opportunity. Some specific words, which can be helpful, are:

- "Please respect my decision to leave."
- "I'd be happy to share my reasons for leaving after I have gone."

Your boss will feel they have much to lose with your resignation. They will be concerned about how the work you have been doing will get done and how they can save face when they have lost a valuable employee. You can help by asking, "How can we make this transition positive?" If possible, share specific ideas for the transition.

Be prepared for various reactions from your managers and colleagues when you announce your resignation. Hopefully, they will express delight that you have this excellent career opportunity. However, since your resignation will catch them by surprise, their initial response may be harmful. This is only natural. You have been a valuable team member, and your departure will leave a hole. However, it won't take long for the people in your best interests to congratulate you and support your decision to enhance your career.

You should also be prepared for the possibility that your employer will ask you to leave immediately. This is an especially likely scenario if you will be joining a competitor. (To be prepared for this scenario, removing personal effects from your office before resigning is a good idea.)

Many companies ask departing employees to give an "exit interview." This meeting is often with someone in the Human Resources department, or it may be with a manager in your department. Every company handles these interviews differently, but the specifics of your resignation (e.g., final paychecks, extension of healthcare coverage, etc.) and your reasons for leaving will likely be covered. You should handle this discussion like the resignation discussion with your boss. Stay positive, focusing on the opportunity ahead rather than specific concerns with your current employer.

What If My Employer Gives Me A Counteroffer?

Your employer may try to convince you to stay. They will appeal to your loyalty, guilt, or vanity to do this. They might even use fear. If they give you a counteroffer or ask you to delay your decision, restate your commitment to the new opportunity.

Counteroffers are flattering but are also dangerous. According to *Business Week*, nine out of ten people who accept a counteroffer are looking again after six months. There are lots of reasons for this.

Here are ten vital reasons for not accepting a counteroffer:

1. Where is the money for the Counter Offer coming from? Is it your next raise early? All companies have strict wage and salary guidelines, which must be followed.

2. You have now informed your employer that you are unhappy. Your loyalty will always be in question from this day on.

3. When promotion time comes around, your employer will remember who was loyal and who wasn't.

4. Once the word gets out, the relationship that you now enjoy with your coworkers will never be the same. You will lose the personal satisfaction of peer-group acceptance.

5. What type of company do you work for if you threaten to resign before they give you what you are worth?

6. Your company will immediately start looking for a new person at a lower starting salary.

7. When times get tough, Your employer will begin the cutback with you first.

8. Accepting a Counteroffer insults your intelligence and a blow to your pride, knowing that you were bought.

9. The circumstances that now cause you to consider a change will repeat themselves in the future, even if you accept a counteroffer.

10. Statistics show that if you accept a Counter Offer, the probability of your voluntarily leaving in (6) six months or being let go within (1) one year is extremely high.

Sample Letter of Resignation

Date

Your Boss
XYZ Widget Company
123 Main Street
Anytown USA

Dear Boss:

Thank you for the opportunities afforded me while at XYZ Company. However, I have accepted and am committed to an opportunity that significantly advances my career. I am excited about this opportunity because_____.

My last day of employment at XYZ Company will be in two weeks, on May 30, 2001. I will make myself available until then to assist in making the transition as smooth as possible. I will summarize the status of all my projects and update my contact list.

As a reminder, after my departure, the company will owe me for last quarter's bonus, two unused vacation days, and five unused sick days.

I wish you and XYZ Company all the best and thank you for your professionalism in supporting my decision.

Sincerely,

You

Chapter 11

New Job Assimilation (On-Boarding)

Executive Quick-Start: The First 100 Days on the Job

In today's breakneck business world, companies demand fast results from every newly hired employee. The traditional long-term "honeymoon" period is a thing of the past. "Hit the ground running" is everyone's mantra. "Faster, cheaper, better, 24/7."

Almost everyone can tell a story about a brilliant, skilled executive promoted to a critical leadership position only to fail. While poor hiring practices or cultural fit may cause some failures, the most significant number is due to poor assimilation of the executive into the team or organization.

Successful assimilation strategies consider the time limitations of today's business world by helping the new leader focus on the best use of their time and talent during this crucial early phase. They create a plan to facilitate quick action for long-term success. A results-based follow-up measurement and feedback process is used to determine the impact of the leader's business objectives. High-impact assimilation goes beyond just creating a plan — but provides ongoing support to get the most sustainable success out of the plan. This process helps keep the leader on track when the "real deal" surfaces and adjustments are required based on new challenges that were not clear at the time of hiring or emerged since then from the rapidly changing world of work.

Assimilating into Your New Position
- Read the new corporate culture.
- Build alliances and influence others.

- Determine and align expectations.
- Focus on early-impact projects.

Typically included in an assimilation strategy is a development plan that surfaces the "skeletons in the closet." If delegating was a problem in the past, it is time to start focusing on offsetting or strengthening that competency rather than waiting until you're settled into your new job. After all, things rarely settle down enough so that you can focus entirely on your development. To succeed, executives need to make development an ongoing process.

According to a report by the Wall Street Journal, there are five general reasons why executives flop in their new jobs. The study concluded that a misstep in any of the following areas often resulted in a "house of cards" effect.

Problems which lead to ineffective leadership can be expensive to correct. The most obvious cost, a severance package, translates into two or more years' salary. Problems such as qualified staff jumping ship, diminished morale, poor strategic positioning, missed opportunities, and tarnished reputations, while less obvious, can result in survival issues for the company.

1. **Confusion or clarity about what their bosses expect of them.**
2. **Failure to build partnerships with peers, subordinates, and direct reports.**
3. **Inability to identify and achieve their top three "most important" objectives**
4. **Lack of political savvy within the organization**
5. **Taking too long to learn the job**

Many cost-conscious organizations recognize the value of having executives get started on the right foot. Companies use one-on-one executive coaching to speed up new job assimilation and prevent early missteps. A personal coach can help the new executive quickly identify job-related competencies necessary for success. Working with the coach, the new executive can develop a targeted improvement plan to fill any identified gaps.

A personal coach can assist a new executive in several other areas as well:

- **Rapidly understanding the overall "big picture" and what is truly valued.**
- **Establishing solid people relationships with managers, peers, and team members.**
- **Identifying "themes," establishing priorities, and developing visible deliverables.**
- **Spotting possible obstacles and how they might be overcome.**
- **Communicating the guiding vision, issues, and priorities and proposing thoughtful, informed actions.**

This quick-start approach for executive assimilation can eliminate "trial and error" assumptions, develop solid alliances with essential stakeholders, learn to respond to new situations in conformity with what already exists, and establish a solid basis for a successful future with the organization. By engaging an executive coach, companies can provide their senior management teams with the most valuable tools to increase their effectiveness and sense of accomplishment.

Boosting your chances of success

Give yourself the best chance of succeeding in a new role. It is essential to realize that assimilation is a two-way process. Successful new hires take ownership of and responsibility for assimilation into a new company and don't leave this in the employer's hands.

Assimilation does not begin only on your first day at a new company. It starts during the interview and the recruitment process. While the initial objective is to get the job, it is equally important to assess what it would be like to work for the company, how people act in the workplace, how employees communicate, and how the work gets done.

Building relationships
The relationships developed at the beginning of a new hire's tenure are critical to the success of assimilation. Look to build relationships inside and outside the company and to develop coaches, sponsors, mentors, and confidants. These relationships will also develop an interest in you and have a vested interest in your success.

Joining a new organization should be an enriching experience – you can start afresh and not repeat past mistakes. As part of your assimilation, build trust and demonstrate trustworthiness. If you say you'll do something, do it. Volunteer to get involved or help others and recognize other people's efforts. Do not be a self-promoter, but keep people informed about your actions. Be a receptive listener, willing to accept feedback.

Have a plan
Develop a plan to map your assimilation and your progress toward targets. Identify thirty-, sixty- and ninety-day plans. Plan to learn, develop, and execute upon your arrival. Study the company history and learn about the business. Know the market and your competition and link this knowledge to your role and responsibilities. Measure your progress against your plan and ask others for feedback.

It is also important to realize that although your first 100 days will probably be the most formative, assimilation never stops, and as your environment changes, you should apply your assimilation principles throughout your career.

Be Popular at Work: Four Steps

For years, we've heard it's more important to be respected than liked. Yet study after study proves conventional wisdom wrong, finding instead that the road to success is more often a series of popularity contests.

Academic research shows that jobs, pay raises, and promotions are more likely to be awarded based on a worker's charisma than their educational background or professional qualifications.

Outplacement firms have found that hiring and firing decisions during corporate downsizing boils down to how well people are liked by their supervisors. It's not enough to do a good job; you have to be likable in the eyes of your employer.

The good news is that being likable is a skill that can be learned. When people encounter you, they subconsciously ask themselves four questions to determine whether they like you. First, they seek friendliness. Then, they ask themselves if you are relevant to them. Next, they ponder whether you have empathy for them. Finally, they ask themselves if you are genuine, authentic, and honest. If the answers to those four questions are positive, you receive a high "Likeability Factor."

Here are four steps to increase "Likeability-Factor."

Step One: Increase Your Friendliness
Your friendliness is a function of your ability to communicate openness and welcome to others. Greet people cheerfully, smile often, and adopt a friendly mindset in which you communicate through positive body language and words.

Step Two: Raise Your Relevance
Your relevance is connecting to others' interests, wants, and needs. The more relevant - the more people like you. Relevance has three levels:

- **Contact**. The odds are your "L Factor" will increase with "functional distance," such as sitting next to someone at a party or living nearby.
- **Mutual Interests.** Having common interests or experiences makes people feel validated and generates a sense of community and personal respect.
- **Value.** Relevance is vital when the value you offer meets another person's wants and needs. This produces positive attitudes in the person's mind and contributes to your allure.

To become more relevant, find ways to connect with the interests and needs of others. Know what they're passionate about outside of work. Be aware of their emotional needs and willing to respond to them.

Step Three: Show Empathy
Your empathy reflects your capacity to see things from another person's point of view and to experience their feelings yourself. When you connect with someone's feelings, and they believe you're "with them," it delivers a psychological hug. Ask yourself, do I:

- Do you know how that person feels about their life situation?
- Understand what it must feel like to perform the person's tasks day after day -- be it caring for an elderly relative at home or managing a heavy workload.
- Do you share the same emotions about critical issues?

By making yourself more emotionally available, your connection with people -- and your likable factor -- will grow dramatically.

Step Four: Keep It Real
Realness is consistency between your beliefs and actions. To be true to yourself and others, you need to:

- Do what you want to be doing in life.

- Live with purpose.
- Commit to the principles of your work.
- Be the same person on the outside as you are on the inside.
- Be direct and honest with others.

The more you live by your values, your perceived realness will elevate. Conversely, if people decide you're not genuine, they will discount your friendliness, relevance, and empathy -- and probably dislike you.

Being likable comes down to creating positive emotional experiences in others. When you make others feel good, they tend to gravitate to you."

Word-of-Mouth Marketing Fuels Success

When Sally is not treated well at the local cleaners, she doesn't go back there and tells others of her unpleasant experience. People talk! They discuss their frustrations, disappointments, poor service, and inadequate products.

Statistics indicate that every unsatisfied customer tells at least eight people about their unpleasant experience. People tend to talk about unsatisfactory service readily, yet what you want is to have them talk about excellent service.

Imagine if every person who came to your center told eight people about how you enhance people's lives daily. The people you serve are your best vehicle for positive word-of-mouth marketing.

Tips for Generating Word-of-Mouth Marketing

1. Create a memorable, easily repeatable value statement. Decide what it is that you want people to say about your center. What do you want people to think of when they think of your center? Make it easy for people to talk about you by giving them the words to say.

2. Provide quality service and, most of all, treat people with respect.
Make sure respect is present in everything you do and say. Respect creates a feeling of honor that nourishes people at the soul level. Communicate your commitment to "respect" by the way that you speak, i.e., "We respect the difficulty you must face when . . ." "We respect your need to . . ." "We want you to feel like you've been treated with the respect you deserve . . ."

3. Ask people to spread the word.
Ask people to help you reach others who can benefit from your services. With some encouragement, individuals will help you spread the word to others throughout the community.

4. Give people something great to talk about.
Do something extraordinary that makes people want to talk. What can you do that will naturally get people talking? It could be a community project, a new service, or an in-house program. Be willing to be creative and do something extraordinary that gets people's attention.

5. Stay in touch with people.
Staying in touch with people increases the chance they will mention and recommend your center to others. There are always plenty of reasons to be in touch. Ensure you don't get too busy to ignore those nudges to call people. Be aware and alert to opportunities to be in touch.

6. Acknowledge people.
Acknowledge people for being clients, contributors, vendors, and community supporters. Make sure that the people in your life realize they contribute to your work. Include people in celebrations and acknowledgments regarding the center, which impacts people's lives.

Does your community know about the value and benefits of your services? If not, they need to, and it is up to you to get the word out. You can initiate a word-of-mouth grapevine that creates positive visibility and exposure. Creating this type of visibility is critical - how can the people who want and need what you have find you?

Maintaining Your Career Momentum

Networking is a natural process of meeting people, making contacts, and building strong professional relationships. It is not a complicated process, yet it is a deliberate process. As humans, we naturally need to be in a relationship with others. It is up to each of us to honor that natural desire to connect, link, and develop camaraderie. There are endless possibilities around you -- people are just waiting for someone to break the ice. Your network can be your most valuable accomplishment in your life. It can be the foundation of support for achievements in all areas of your life--guaranteed!

- **Continuously survey your professional environment.**
- **Occasionally redefine your professional objective.**
- **Always have a communications strategy.**
- **Manage your professional reputation.**

Use People's Names
Pay attention as people introduce themselves so you can address them by name during the current conversation and increase your chances of remembering their names later.

Power Networking: Turning Contacts into Business
Successful people use networking skills to market themselves, generate business, and solve daily problems! By all means, keep your Network alive and nurtured. You never know when to tap into your essential career contacts again.

Preparation for a Networking Event
Learn everything about the event -- activities, attendees, schedule, etc. Then, determine what will make you feel comfortable: Should you go with someone you know who's also attending? Is it appropriate to bring a friend, associate, or client? Would it be more profitable for you to be

an attendee or an exhibitor?

Identify the People You Want to Visit

A convention is an excellent opportunity to strengthen existing relationships and expand your network. Consider who will likely be there and mentally note the new contacts and reconnections you want to make.

Participation in Networking Events

- **Get Involved**

    One way to put yourself at ease is to give yourself something to do. Volunteering gives you a job, gets you involved, and naturally connects you with other volunteers and participants.

- **Focus on Others**

    Rather than worrying about what you will say, focus on what others say. When you focus on something or someone other than yourself, your self-consciousness will disappear, and others will be more likely to remember and appreciate you.

- **Listen and Gather Information**

    Good conversationalists know the importance of active listening. It conveys a natural interest in others and enables you to be more aware of what to say and talk about to keep the conversation flowing.

- **Use People's Names**

    Pay attention as people introduce themselves so you can address them by name during the current conversation and increase your chances of remembering their names later.

- **Move on Graciously**

    A networking event is a place to meet and mingle. Yet, people often feel uncomfortable ending a conversation to mingle and talk with others. Just be gracious with a closing comment such as

"Nice to meet you. Have a good afternoon." "Good luck with your new venture."

- **Exchange Business Cards**
  Business cards are best exchanged for reasons such as "I'll call about scheduling a time to get together for lunch" or "Give me a card, and I'll send that information to you tomorrow."

- **Relax, Have Fun, and Enjoy Yourself**
  People often get uptight about attending networking events because they feel they must find a new prospect, make a sale, or accomplish some significant goal. Networking is meant to be fun. Relax—the more at ease you feel, the more likely you'll make some good, solid contacts. The goal shouldn't be the quantity of interactions but the quality.

ADAPTABILITY

It's been said, adaptability is one of the most valuable lessons in any career. In a fast-changing world, being open to new ideas, technologies, and ways of doing things is essential for long-term success.

Chapter 12

Lessons Learned on the Career Path to Success

"Manage Your Mindset to Manage Your Time." Mark James

28 Tips For Working Smarter, Not Harder

Are you working longer hours but getting less done? Are you being asked to do more in less time? Beginning to feel like a hostage at work? Productivity problems can make you feel incredibly stressed--and then you're just spinning your wheels. But wait! There is help. You can use your mind. You can soon be winning the mental game of personal productivity. Peak-performing sales professionals work smarter, not harder. They want to achieve the maximum in business and still have a life.

Here's how you can do that too:

1. Start the day being very clear about what you want to accomplish-personally and professionally.

2. Once a quarter, perform a time analysis on your entire week at home and work.

3. Make a list of the things you should avoid doing today--and then don't do them.

4. Don't strive for perfection in everything; perfection doesn't matter with all tasks.

5. Sweep your mind clear of clutter before you engage your brain on a project.

6. Set boundaries and limits to position yourself for balanced time management.

7. Schedule "real-life" personal appointments in your organizer or daily

planner in advance and adhere to them.

8. Ask yourself, "Am I managing my time well enough to allow me the freedom to enjoy life after work?"

9. At the end of the day, review what you have accomplished and compliment and reward yourself for suitable tasks completed.

10. Motivate yourself for good work by promising yourself exercise or a break reward once you achieve a level of excellence in a task.

11. Stay conscious of your time management choices during the day.

12. Compartmentalize your tasks so you focus on one task at a time.

13. Build up mental momentum with each successful task completed so you proudly gain energy as you go through your day.

14. Build variety into your schedule so you have engaging activities to look forward to during less exciting tasks.

15. Create positive tension and an urgency to get things done faster by having more to do than you can achieve--but keep your focus on the here and now.

16. Be selective. Don't classify too many things as priorities or urgent.

17. Know what to say no to and stick to your decisions.

18. Always ask yourself, "Is this the best use of my time?"

19. Visualize yourself succeeding before every task. Hint: Start with the end in mind!

20. Don't be continually reactive to your electronic tools--don't reflexively retrieve them when they come in--collect voicemail and email at specified times to maintain uninterrupted focus.

21. Plan quiet time for thinking, planning, and analyzing.

22. Create your own custom "best time management program"--don't

use someone else.

23. Ask yourself, "Is what I am doing right now making a difference?"

24. Do things today that will give you leveraged advancements in your work weeks from now.

25. Systematize regular, repetitious tasks by setting up more innovative processes.

26. Build team delegation and support from associates, friends, and family to take the pressure off yourself.

27. Lower your expectations of perfection, and don't expect 100% completion of your to-do list each day--carry some over for another day.

28. Review your values every quarter to know what is essential to you and how to plan your time.

Winning the mental game of personal productivity is all about being intentional in the planning and execution of your day. It's about using your superior powers of mind to creatively solve the daily challenges you face to maximize your value every moment.

The Unwritten Rules of Management
Master these mental strategies on this list and watch your productivity soar.

1. Learn to say "I don't know" if used when appropriate; it should be used often.
2. Getting into something is easier than getting out of it.
3. You may not be doing well if you are not criticized.
4. Look for what is missing. Many know how to improve what's there; few can see what isn't.
5. Presentation rule: When something appears on a slide presentation, assume the world knows about it and deal with it accordingly.

The Recruiter Mindset

6. Work for a boss for whom you can tell it like it is. Remember, you can't pick your family, but you can pick your boss.
7. Constantly review the developments to ensure the actual benefits are what they should be. Avoid Newton's Law.
8. Give them your best efforts, however menial and trivial your early assignments may appear.
9. Persistence or tenacity is the dispassion to persevere despite difficulties, discouragement, or indifference. Don't be known as a good starter or a poor finisher.
10. Don't wait for others to do your project: go after them and ensure it gets done.
11. Confirm the instructions you give others and their commitments in writing. Don't assume it will get done!
12. Don't be timid: Speak up, express yourself, and promote your ideas.
13. Practice shows that those who speak the most knowingly and confidently often end up with the assignment to get the job done.
14. Strive for brevity and clarity in oral and written reports. Brevity is the key to excellent communication.
15. Be extremely careful in the accuracy of your statements.
16. Don't overlook the fact you are working for the boss. Keep him or her informed. Whatever the boss wants, within the bounds of honesty, ethics and integrity
17. Promises, schedules, and estimates are essential for a well-run business. You must make promises – don't lean on the often-used phrase: "I can't estimate it because it depends on uncertain factors. "
18. Never direct a complaint to the top; a serious offense is to "cc" a person's boss on a copy of a complaint before the person can respond.

19. Remember to professionally represent the company when interacting with customers, prospects, vendors, and clients.
20. Cultivate the habit of boiling matters down to the simplest terms: the preverbal "elevator speech" is the best way.
21. Don't get excited in engineering emergencies: keep your feet on the ground.
22. Cultivate the habit of making quick, clean–cut decisions.
23. When making decisions, the "pros" are much easier to deal with than the "cons." Your boss wants to see both.
24. Don't ever lose your sense of humor.
25. Have fun at what you do. It will be reflected in your work. No one likes a grump except another grump.
26. Treat your company's name as if it were your own.
27. Beg for the bad news.
28. You remember 1/3 of what you read, ½ of what people tell you, but 100% of what you feel.
29. If you don't know the answer, conduct "accelerated research" and get back to the person immediately.
30. When facing issues of problems that are becoming drawn–out, "short them to ground."
31. When faced with decisions, look at them as if you were one level up in the organization. Your perspective will change quickly.
32. A person who is nice to you but rude to the waiter or others is not nice. (This rule never fails.)
33. Never be afraid to try something new. Remember, an amateur built an ark that survived a flood, while a large group of professionals built the Titanic.

Before we close the book on these unwritten rules, here is an additional observation on leadership. People sometimes ask me what I believe are the essential qualities of leadership.

To me, the qualities of great leaders boil down to:

> Confidence
>
> Dedication
>
> Adaptability
>
> Resourcefulness
>
> Motivation
>
> Honesty
>
> Ethics
>
> Integrity
>
> Trust
>
> Love
>
> Respect

Bonus Chapter

One Person's Journey

Mike has been looking for a job since he was laid off from his SVP Sales position for a large manufacturing company three months ago. When he realized he wouldn't land a new role quickly, he followed a friend's advice and engaged a career transition coach to learn how to conduct a professional job search campaign.

Initially, he was over-confident about his chances of landing quickly. After all, he made significant contributions for years and had great reviews, and the results outlined in a good (but not great) resume.

Additionally, Mike believed getting laid off did not have the stigma it was decades ago. Companies restructure, merge, and get acquired; top leadership changes and brings in their people. Executive's salary outgrow their jobs, and the deck chairs get rearranged.

Mike soon realized that being "optimistic and in the market" isn't a strategy. His optimism changed to hope. I hope that I can land a job soon. He would get a few interviews, attention, and job offers, which did not happen. Hope can be good if you do something with it, but hope is not a strategy.

Mike figured he would add the green banner "Open to Work" to his LinkedIn profile headshot photo. Little did he know that this would only brand him as anxious, needy, and distant to hiring managers, especially recruiters.

Mike also spent much of his time scouring the internet job boards—I call this looking at the candy in the window. This represents a tiny percentage of job search success. Online job posts and applying to the major job boards are likely to be an exercise in futility.

Mike was getting depressed and knew he needed professional coaching and guidance. He researched and hired a career transition coach, who helped him understand that he had to become an expert in explaining how his skills could move a company's needle.

Mike's career transition coach advised him to conduct "Informational Interviews with trusted friends, peers, and leaders he has known throughout his career." His coach helped Mike set goals to reach out and establish relationships with ten executive recruiters every week. This recruiter strategy paid dividends in the long run.

He gradually realized that most executives can relay what they have done but are not skilled at sharing why a company should care. He learned that creating a Value Proposition Story involves addressing company goals and objectives by sharing his past comparable accomplishments and solutions.

He learned the candidate's value proposition story needs to be established and should be what people hear from you when interacting with you. To be effective, it needs to be clearly stated on your resume. Unlike a manager-level resume, an executive-level resume is not simply a list of titles, companies, and duties. The executive's resume weaves a story of metrics and accomplishments that support the value proposition story. Executives in demand understand how to share their value proposition and have personal marketing materials that reflect their executive status.

Mike learned to stop hoping the other person would connect the dots about how he could help. He learned to talk about his value in a focused and transparent way, and his resume supported that story. This individualized approach to demonstrating value makes all the difference in an executive-level search.

HIRE Consulting Services (HCS) Career Coaching for Executives and Professionals in Career Transition

Do you need coaching with conducting a professional job search campaign and managing your career path?

To schedule a 30-minute consultation with HCS, email your resumé and cover letter to info@HireConsulting.com. Please include your two best days and times to talk by phone.
We will reply with a preferred time to schedule the appointment.

==

HCS Published Book Online Resource Documents

The Recruiter Mindset (2024), **The Interview Mindset** (2022), and **Keys to the C SUITE** (2018) reference several documents that are available to download for your job search on the **Hire Consulting Services** (HCS) website link below:
https://hireconsulting.com/career-transition-resource-documents/

==

Companies and Organizations that are interested in learning more about HCS Strategic Recruiting Solutions, Talent Selection, and Optimization with The Predictive Index Behavior Assessment, please get in touch with HCS directly:

HIRE Consulting Services:
- ▶ 760-230-4301 (San Diego Office)
- ▶ Info@HireConsulting.com
- ▶ https://hireconsulting.com/contact/

The Recruiter Mindset

About Mark James, CPC

Mark James, CPC, is the Founder and President of **Hire Consulting Services (HCS)** in San Diego, CA. He is a Certified Personnel Consultant (CPC) and founded HCS in 1999. He has provided executive career coaching and executive search recruiting services for over 25 years. Mark has screened and interviewed hundreds of management executives and professionals for critical positions, leading to the placement of many executives in various disciplines and industries for small to large companies. He has been a Certified Partner with The Predictive Index since 2016.

Additionally, Mark is the author of two best-selling books; *"The Interview Mindset" (2022)* and *"Keys to the C Suite," (2018).* He excels in coaching business professionals and executives who are changing jobs or transitioning careers. He provides a unique and candid perspective for people in career transition and those needing to improve their focus on managing their career path. He delivers a successful career management coaching process, expert mock interview training, and honest expert advice by guiding clients to execute a professional job search campaign strategy. Since 2005, Mark has hosted and facilitated the monthly CareerNET Networking Meetings in Southern California. Mark has been blogging since 2006, called **The HIRE Report Blog**.

The Recruiter Mindset

www.ingramcontent.com/pod-product-compliance
Lightning Source LLC
Chambersburg PA
CBHW050108230526
45470CB00004B/1732